Belie

A Layman's Reflection on the Gospel According to St. John

Philip L. Yuson

Dedicated to:

My wife Marie
My children Pauline and Joseph

and all those who helped me in my faith journey

Table of Contents

Foreword..1

Acknowledgments..5

Introduction..7

The Beginning..11

The New Temple...17

Born of the Spirit...21

Worship in Spirit and Truth.................................25

Jesus: Equal to the Father...................................31

The Father's Will..35

Who is Jesus?..41

Slavery and Freedom..45

New Eyes to See Jesus..49

Abundant Life in Jesus...55

The Resurrection...59

The Glory Begins 65

Prepared for Glory..71

Trust in God...75

Stand Firm in Jesus..81

Victory of Jesus...85

Infinite Glory...89

Jesus is in Control...95

King of the Jews..103

Joy after Sorrow..111

Follow Jesus...121

Epilogue...131

Foreword

This is a lay person's reflections of the Gospel according to St. John. So what are my credentials for writing this?

The only credential I claim in writing this is I am baptized in Jesus. Like everyone baptized in Jesus, I am called to share in his prophetic ministry - to speak God's word and to preach the good news.

As a baptized Catholic, it is also my duty to give glory to God, since this is the purpose for which everyone is created.

I want to show how God can use someone like me to preach his good news - all for his glory. This is the main reason for writing this reflection.

The Book of Numbers tells of an instance where a donkey spoke God's word. I want to show people that God can also speak through ordinary and sinful people like me.

What a great God we serve!

SCRIPTURE IN MY LIFE

From my youth until my early adult years, I knew the Lord intellectually. I knew him through catechism and theology classes in elementary and high school. I knew him but I never really KNEW him.

I could give the right answers to the questions, but I could not say who he was for me. But the Lord is good. Through all these, he prepared me for the moment, when I would make a decision to say *"Yes"* to him, to accept his invitation.

So began my search for him in scripture. Through scripture, I learned about the real Jesus - not the Jesus seen on television or movies, since these were other people's views of who Jesus was. I got to know who Jesus was to me. I had to answer the question Jesus posed to the apostles at Caesarea Philippi, *"who do you say I am"*.

This is why scripture is very important in my life. It has given me comfort, courage and strength throughout the years. It made me know who Jesus is to me.

The journey in reading and loving scripture was difficult. The hardest part was the start. I could not understand what I was reading and nothing would sink in. By constantly reading scripture, even when I did not understand, God revealed himself to me.

GOD REVEALS TO INFANTS

Jesus said, *"I thank you, Father, Lord of heaven and earth, that you hid these things from the wise and understanding, and revealed them to infants. Yes, Father, for so it was well-pleasing in your sight."* Matthew 11:25-26.

If we take Jesus seriously on what he said, then scripture is easy to understand. Since the Father loves everyone, he wants to reveal himself to everyone! This includes infants!

Therefore, the word of God was written in a way so simple that children could understand. The problem with not understanding scripture is not that it is too complicated. The problem with understanding scripture is it is too simple and I complicate it!

By reading it through my own lens, I could not understand it. But when I took the word as it is, emptied my mind of my preconceived ideas about Jesus and just let him reveal himself to me, then everything slowly made sense.

God's Goodness

While scripture led me back to Jesus, the Eucharist made me decide to come back to his Church. It was my moments before the Lord in the Blessed Sacrament that led me back to him through his Mother. I am convinced he is the Bread of Life who came down from heaven - to be with me always.

Through these years of my journey in faith, the Lord led me to know him in other ways. He led me to communities that preached his word. He led me to seminars that deepened my knowledge about him.

As I got more involved in his Church, I met people who turned away from their old life for a life with Jesus. This made me look at my faith and think of my relationship with my Lord.

As I continued in my faith journey, I was able to learn more about the faith. All these have deepened my love for the Lord, his Mother, the saints and his Church.

My training in a technical field also provided me with the skills and tools for the research needed to study scripture. These have taught me to be discriminating in my research materials and also on how to use the tools available.

All these form a whole person - me! And it just shows God can use anyone for his glory if that person is willing and open to him.

These Reflections

The reflections written here were the result of my prayers.

The prayers in this book are my response to God's revelation at this point in my life. Hopefully, they will be useful to you also.

I used multiple translations for my study, most especially the Jerusalem Bible and the Douay-Rheims Bible. However, for copyright reasons, verses quoted in this book are taken from the World English Bible (WEB). For more information about the WEB, you can visit: *http://ebible.org/bible/WEB/*.

DISCLAIMER

I want to clearly state I am not a saint. My ambition is to be one - even if not a canonized one - so I can live with my God for all eternity. What is a saint but someone who is with God. I want to go to heaven that is why I want to be a saint.

I echo St. Paul's prayer in Philippians 3:11-12, *"Not that I have already obtained, or am already made perfect; but I press on, if it is so that I may take hold of that for which also I was taken hold of by Christ Jesus. Brothers, I don't regard myself as yet having taken hold, but one thing I do. Forgetting the things which are behind, and stretching forward to the things which are before, I press on toward the goal for the prize of the high calling of God in Christ Jesus."*

SUBMISSION TO THE CHURCH

Lastly, the views expressed in this book are my own opinions. If there are errors, these are my own and I submit these writings to the full wisdom and authority of the Church my Lord built on Peter. If you find any errors, please feel free to let me know.

May the Father bless you and may he be glorified in all we do, through Jesus Christ our Lord.

Acknowledgments

Although I wrote this book, I believe it is the product of many people - especially those who led me to my current state in faith.

I was formed first and foremost by my parents and siblings and my elementary and high school communities. Although my early life was not filled with faith, the experiences I had built a solid foundation that would be the basis of my faith.

As I grew older, I searched for the Lord. Many people helped me through my search, from the anonymous person who handed me the New Testament, to people who preached God's word on the buses that I took on my way from work, to the friend who patiently led me back to Jesus and his Church, to the spiritual directors and pastors who were patient during the early stages of my faith, all these people made a mark in my life. Their lives and examples made me desire to seek Jesus and build my life on the solid Rock.

As I continued in my faith journey, I thank those who patiently gave me opportunities to grow and spread the word of God: from my home parish of St. Gabriel in Kalookan, Philippines; to the Genesis Catholic Community in Jakarta, Indonesia (http://www.genesis.faithweb.com); to my home parish of St. Andrew's Cathedral in Victoria, BC (http://www.standrewscathedral.com); and to the El Shaddai Victoria Outreach.

All these opportunities to speak about Jesus allowed me to know him more.

Also to all those confessors and pastors God has graciously sent to me - I thank the Lord for them. Their wisdom led me straight when I got lost or when I am distressed.

Of course, to my own family, my wife and children who continue to be so patient with my faults - I thank God for giving you to me.

Lastly, for those who reviewed my book and gave comments, who choose to remain anonymous, thank you.

May the Lord bless you and lead you to the life he has planned for you.

Philip L. Yuson
Easter 2008

6

Introduction

Tradition tells us the Gospel According to St. John was written by John the Apostle sometime towards the end of the first century. The author referred to himself as the disciple whom Jesus loved. He is sometimes referred as the Beloved Disciple.

ONE GOSPEL

There is only one gospel. It is the gospel of Jesus Christ. What is commonly known as the Gospel of John is technically, the Gospel According to John. It is not John's good news, but it is John's version of the good news.

However, since it is tedious to say *"the Gospel According to John"*, some people, including myself in this book, would say, John's gospel. This is one thing to keep in mind: although I say this is John's gospel, what I mean is John's version of the gospel.

A lot of people say John's gospel shows a divine Jesus. I agree with this. However, for me it also shows a very human Jesus. It shows a Jesus who got tired, a Jesus who wept and a Jesus who died. It is through the tired and thirsty Jesus that we see him as the source of Living Water. It is through the Jesus who wept that we see his power over death. It is through the Jesus who died that we see his divinity. This reinforces our belief that Jesus is fully human and fully divine.

THE JEWS: GOD'S CHOSEN PEOPLE

Another thing to note about this gospel is John often referred to the enemies of Jesus as the Jews. This came from the conflicts between the Christians and the Jewish leaders during his time. So when John spoke of Jews in his gospel, he was referring to the Jewish leaders during his time. Sadly, throughout history, many people used this as an excuse to persecute God's chosen people.

Historically, the Jews are the descendants of Abraham. Their ancestor is one of the sons of Israel, Judah. Jesus himself was a Jew. His first apostles were Jews and the majority, if not all, of his early disciples were Jews. Jesus had Jewish friends like Martha, Mary and Lazarus. Even at the trial of Jesus, some Jewish leaders came to his defense. Likewise, two Jewish leaders came to bury Jesus. The first witness to the resurrection was a Jewish woman.

It is through this context that one has to read this gospel. The Catholic Church teaches that the Jews are our elder brothers in faith and as such, they deserve our respect and gratitude. Jesus said, *"Salvation comes from the Jews."* Without them, we would not have salvation. We owe our salvation to them.

DIFFERENT PERSPECTIVE

One of the interesting things about this gospel is it shows Jesus speaking about something from one perspective and his listeners interpreting it from a different perspective.

When Jesus spoke figuratively, his listeners interpreted it literally. And when he spoke literally, his listeners would interpret it figuratively or wrongly interpret it literally.

GOD'S LOVE

When I first read this gospel, I found it quite hard to understand. I liked Matthew better since it had more practical applications to life. However, as I came to read John's gospel several times, I found praying over it gave me a deeper insight into who Jesus is.

John's version unmistakably speaks of God's love. One sees God's love through the words and actions of Jesus. To get the most out of this, one should spend time reflecting on the words and focusing on the person of Jesus and the Father.

Jesus said, *"Whoever sees me has seen the Father."* Looking at Jesus will give an idea of who the Father is.

Purpose of this Book

The purpose of these reflections is to assist you in reading this version of the gospel. I hope this will lead you to a deeper understanding of the gospel and eventually to a deeper understanding of the person of Jesus.

Scripture reading requires time and effort. There are no shortcuts.

St. Teresa of Avila compared prayer to carrying water. One has to labor to bring water up from the well manually. Another way is by using a pulley. The best way of getting water is from rain coming from heaven.

May this short book be the pulley that helps you draw the Living Water out of the well and prepare you to enjoy the rain God will send. May it lead you to a deeper relationship with Jesus. May it prepare you to receive the abundant water God will give you from heaven through Jesus our Lord.

Chapter 1

The Beginning

The gospel begins by showing clearly Jesus is God. He was from the beginning. John described Jesus as the light shining in the darkness. Darkness had no hold on him. He always triumphs over darkness. Even at this point, John showed the gospel as a battle between good and evil, between light and darkness. In this battle, the light always wins over the darkness.

Those in the light, those who chose to believe in Jesus, will have the right to be children of God. In John's gospel, the word "*believe*" occurs more than 80 times. The word does not mean intellectual knowledge or a certainty that God exists. It is instead, confidence in his word, to be so convinced he speaks the truth and respond in obedience and in trust.

The gospel also shows God becoming man. By becoming man, God began his redemption of all creation. To prepare people for his coming, John the Baptist preached repentance and showed people who this God made man was. Many people thought John the Baptist was the Messiah. But he clearly denied this and said his role was to prepare the way for the Messiah. He knew what his position was with regard to God.

THE LAMB OF GOD

John the Baptist's description of Jesus as the "*Lamb of God*" foretold the role of Jesus. Jesus was to be the sacrifice to pay for the sins of all creation. With this, John the Baptist was saying redemption had started. It would happen and nothing could stop it.

Although God became man and he owns everything, the world could not recognize nor receive him.

Only those born of God can see his glory. God's glory is full of grace and truth. Those who receive him (take hold of him) are given the right to be his children. To take hold of Jesus is to possess him. This implies an action is required from the person. To receive Jesus is to reach out and take. It is a personal decision and action. Jesus will not come in unless invited. We must take hold of him so he will come to us.

Since Jesus is the Son, those who believe in him will also share the same rights Jesus has before the Father. Jesus is God. He is the Light who enlightens everyone. By enlightening everyone, he gives them the ability to see God.

> *Lord, may I see you as you are. Open my eyes so I can see you as the true God who takes away, not only the sin of the world, but more specifically, who takes away my sins. You are the one who frees me.*

Even at the beginning of his gospel, John pointed to the death of Jesus. Jesus was the Son of God who would die and rise again to save all creation. When Jesus approached John the Baptist, the Baptist pointed him out to his disciples. One thing to note here is while the other gospels mentioned the baptism of Jesus, John did not mention it in his gospel.

WHAT ARE YOU LOOKING FOR?

Two of the Baptist's disciples came to Jesus. These two were Andrew and the Beloved Disciple. As they approached him, Jesus turned and saw them and asked, *"What are you looking for?"*

This question was not only directed to the disciples. It is directed to everyone, including you!

Indeed, *"What are you looking for?"* What do you want from Jesus? This is the time to tell him. If there is a void in your life, tell Jesus about this void. Only he can fill it. If you are distressed, tell Jesus how you feel. He is here, speak to him.

Everyone is looking for something to satisfy them. Years ago, I too searched for something that would give meaning to my life. Yet, nothing did, until I accepted Jesus and experienced the power of the Living God.

> *Jesus, your words are true. You ask me what I want. I want you Lord. You alone can give me life.*

COME, AND SEE JESUS

The disciples wanted to know where he was staying. Jesus invited them to *"Come, and see."*

Jesus also invites us to come and see him. This invitation welcomes us to experience him; to stay with him. In this chapter, the two disciples stayed with Jesus for the night. They learned where he lived. They talked to him. They saw him. They heard him speak. In short, they experienced him!

> *Lord God, I constantly search for you. Do not hide yourself from me, but in your mercy, hear me. You are all I need. You are all I want. I am looking for you. May I hear you call me, inviting me to come and see you so I may truly know you.*

THE FIRST DISCIPLES

The next day, Andrew brought his brother Simon to Jesus. Jesus immediately renamed him *Peter*. Since this gospel was originally written in Greek, the name Peter is a translation of the Aramaic word *Kephas* which means *Rock*. By changing Simon's name, Jesus changed Simon's destiny. He was no longer Simon the fisherman. He was Simon the Rock. Jesus wanted Simon to be the foundation of his Church. Even at that time, before the start of his ministry, Jesus was building his Church. He was laying the foundation of his Church. The Church was part of the plan for redemption.

Further on, Jesus saw Philip. Of the first disciples, only Philip was personally called by Jesus. The others either approached Jesus or were brought to him.

Philip found Nathanael and told him that he had seen the Messiah. When Nathanael voiced his doubt, Philip replied, *"Come and see."* These were the same words Jesus used to invite the first two disciples.

To experience Jesus, one has to come and see him. One must experience him. Faith is not based on intellectual knowledge. It is to be experienced. One must have a personal relationship with God for one's faith to be real.

When Nathanael came to Jesus, Jesus said about him *"Behold, an Israelite indeed, in whom is no deceit!"* Nathanael was surprised and asked how Jesus knew him. Jesus told Nathanael he saw him under the fig tree even before Philip called him. When Jesus said this, Nathanael immediately said, *"Rabbi, you are the Son of God, You are the King of Israel!"* With this, Nathanael believed Jesus and became his disciple.

Notice the play on words. Jesus called Nathanael an Israelite and Nathanael in turn called Jesus the King of Israel. An Israelite was professing his king.

To understand this, one must know a little history of the people of Israel. Jacob had twelve sons. God later changed Jacob's name to *Israel*. God promised to be with the descendants of Israel. When the descendants of Israel came back to the Promised Land, the land was divided among the descendants of ten sons and two grandsons of Israel. Each of these formed a tribe.

The descendants of one of the sons, Levi, were not given any portion of the land. They were to live among the other tribes as priests.

Some time in history, the ten northern tribes separated from the two southern tribes. The northern tribes formed the kingdom of Israel and the two southern tribes formed the kingdom of Judah. The Jews are descendants of the tribe of Judah.

So Jesus did not only come for the descendants of Judah. He came for the descendants of Judah and his brothers, for all the children of Israel.

Jesus said, *"Hereafter you will see heaven opened, and the angels of God ascending and descending on the Son of Man."*

By saying this, Jesus brought Nathanael back to the dream of Jacob. Early in his life, Jacob tricked his brother and was running away from him. As he was fleeing, he slept and had a dream. He saw a ladder from the earth to heaven with angels ascending and descending. With this, Jesus was saying he was the new Israel - the fulfillment of God's promise.

Jesus, you are the King of Israel. May I follow you and live for you.

Chapter 2

The New Temple

This chapter narrates the first sign Jesus did: he changed water into wine. The water was used for washing. It was not used for drinking. This sign showed Jesus was making something new. Jesus was taking what was not fit for drinking into something that would not only be fit for drinking, but used for celebration.

Redemption is not fixing something broken. Redemption is making something new.

Mary and the First Miracle

This sign happened through Mary, the mother of Jesus. Even if it was not yet the time for him to reveal himself, Jesus performed this sign for her. His mother told the servants to do what Jesus said.

When the servants took the wine, was it still water? This verse seems to imply that it was so. Verse 9 says, *"the servants who had drawn the water knew."*

Credit the sign then to the faith of the servants. Even if what they were giving the governor of the feast was dirty water to drink, they still did it for the simple reason that Jesus told them. This shows redemption is possible ONLY when one is obedient to Jesus. A new creation is possible only by obeying Jesus.

With the changing of water to wine, Jesus changed the water of repentance to the Spirit of power and joy.

THE TEMPLE OF HIS BODY

When Jesus went to the Temple, he drove out all the merchants and animals. Confronted by the authorities, he told them to *"Destroy this temple, and in three days I will raise it up... But he spoke of the temple of his body."*

The temple of his body was not only his physical body, but his Church. At the death of Jesus, the leaders did not only destroy THE Temple of God. They destroyed the Son of God himself. He redeemed the Temple by raising up his own body. Since the Church is the Body of Jesus, his resurrection made perfect the Temple. The old Temple was made new with the creation of the New Jerusalem - the Church - the community of believers.

By redeeming the Temple, Jesus made all things new. He created a new nation for his chosen people. This nation is the Church, where Simon is Peter - the Rock.

At the end of Chapter 1, Jesus claimed to be the new Israel. The old Israel was established through Jacob and his twelve sons. The new Israel was established through Jesus and his twelve apostles. The old Israel had a physical temple. The new Israel has a spiritual temple.

This is why in the letter to the Hebrews, the author said we are *"citizens of heaven"*. Just as the old Temple was the symbol of God's presence, the Church is the symbol of Christ's presence. She is also called the Body of Christ.

> *Lord, thank you for giving me your Church. Thank you for bringing me to your Church. May I treasure this gift and may I see you in your Church. Build your Church O Lord and make her holy.*

BELIEVING IN SCRIPTURE

When Jesus rose from the dead, *"they believed the Scripture and the word which Jesus had said."* This is the second instance when the word *believe* is mentioned in this chapter. The first was after the miracle at Cana. In the first case, they believed in Jesus. This time, they believed in scripture and his word.

Our faith is based on our belief in Jesus. Faith in Jesus is the key to life. We can only believe in scripture if we believe in Jesus. We can only believe in Jesus when we believe his word.

> *Lord, teach me to believe in you - to trust in you.*

The author ended this chapter by saying Jesus "*knew everyone.*" He is God so he knows everyone. He knows me. He knows you. He knows us more than we can ever know ourselves.

The author also said Jesus "*didn't need for anyone to testify concerning man; for he himself knew what was in man.*" Jesus knows everything. He knows our deepest fears and doubts. He knows our strengths and weaknesses. The good news is he also has the power to do something about them. He changed water into wine. He is God and therefore, able to help us overcome these and lead us to victory.

Jesus said, "*Destroy this temple, and in three days I will raise it up... But he spoke of the temple of his body.*" As members of the Church, we are the temples of his body.

You are the temple of the Holy Spirit. Jesus can destroy the old person: the fearful person, the doubting person, the weak person. By destroying it, he will perfect you and make you new. The resurrection of Jesus proves this. There is victory in following Jesus. Believe in Scripture and believe in his word. Believe in Jesus.

> *Lord, here is my body. Take it and change it. Make it holy my Lord. May I live for the glory of your name.*

Chapter 3

Born of the Spirit

Nicodemus was a leader of the people. He came to Jesus at night. Despite his knowledge and learning of the Law and scripture, he could not understand Jesus. He was still in the dark, symbolized by his coming in the night.

To understand Jesus, one must be born anew or born from above. To be born anew means to be a new person, to have a new perspective, a new way of thinking, a new way of life. It is one where things are seen through the eyes of God and not through human eyes.

> *Lord, here I am. Give me new perspective every day. Give me new eyes every day. Give me new life every day. I want to be born anew so I can know you more.*

KNOWING JESUS

Understanding Jesus is a gift from God. We can only understand Jesus when we are born of the Spirit. To be born of the Spirit means one is led by the Spirit.

Jesus compared the Spirit to the wind. We know the wind blows but we do not know where it comes from or where it is going. Similarly, the one born of the Spirit is one who is totally docile to the Spirit - totally open to him. Only by being so, can the Spirit lead us to full knowledge of Jesus.

For the Spirit to move, one must believe in Jesus. To believe is to know with conviction even without proof. It is to trust in the Spirit. Wherever the Spirit leads, one goes, trusting fully that he leads to a deeper understanding of Jesus. This obedience and gentleness to the Spirit leads to eternal life. Eternal life is believing in Jesus. Believing in Jesus is saying YES to him. It results in trusting in him, going where he leads and following him - even if one does not know nor understand.

> *Holy Spirit, come and renew me. Change my perspective so I may see things through the eyes of the Father. I want to know Jesus. Reveal him to me.*

LOOK AT THE LIFTED JESUS

Jesus said, *"As Moses lifted up the serpent in the wilderness, even so must the Son of Man be lifted up, that whoever believes in him should not perish, but have eternal life."*

In that Old Testament episode, the children of Israel were attacked by serpents and died when they were bitten by the serpents. God told Moses to make a brazen image of the serpent and put it on a pole and those who were bitten would not die if they looked at it.

To live, the children of Israel had to look at what caused their death.

Similarly with us, we look at the lifted Jesus and we will not die. St. Paul says in 2 Corinthians 5:21, *"For him who knew no sin he made to be sin on our behalf; so that in him we might become the righteousness of God."*

When I look at sin, confront it and stare it in the eye, and I lift it up, uncover it, raise it up and confess it - that is when I shall have life. To be born of the Spirit, there has to be repentance first. Repentance is our way of telling God we seek his forgiveness.

There is no rebirth without repentance because we cannot receive forgiveness if we do not want it.

Born In the Spirit

The next step is to choose between lies and the truth. The issue is not which one we choose. Those in the Spirit will always choose and seek the truth. The problem with lies is they look like the truth. Even with a sincere heart, one can unknowingly be misled by a lie.

To be born in the Spirit, one must discern between the truth and the lie. This is possible only with the help of the Holy Spirit. One of the gifts of the Holy Spirit is the gift of discernment.

> *Lord, let me choose you and you alone. Help me to distinguish the truth and the lie. Let me reject the lie and embrace the truth. Guide me Jesus. Holy Spirit, lead me to the truth.*

Jesus must Increase

John the Baptist knew where he stood before Jesus. His mission was done so he had to fade to the background. His disciples did not want that. They wanted John to still be in the limelight. But John knew when Jesus came he must decrease and Jesus must increase.

To be born of the Spirit is to let Jesus take over. He must increase and I must decrease. I must speak HIS words. I must do HIS will. I must share HIS love. What matters is Jesus - his words, his actions, his will, his power, his mercy and his love.

> *Indeed Lord, take over my life. I must decrease and you must increase.*

Chapter 4

Worship in Spirit and Truth

This chapter begins with Jesus and his disciples entering a Samaritan town called Sychar. Jesus was tired and he sat down by the well. The evangelist was very careful to note the humanity of Jesus - he got tired. It was noon, the hottest time of the day, and a Samaritan woman came.

The town, Sychar, was named after a strong alcoholic drink. In this town of a *strong alcoholic drink*, Jesus was asking for water. In Chapter 2, he changed water to wine. In this chapter, he was looking for water in *"wine"*. From a place with no wine to a place with too much *"wine"*.

The people in the town were *"drunk"*. The woman was *"drunk"*. When she came to the well, Jesus asked her for water. She could not give it because all she had was strong wine. Her pride was the strong wine.

> *Lord, give me the Living Water. Fill me with this water so I may not be full of myself. I want to be filled with you Lord. Refresh me Jesus.*

THE LIVING WATER

Jesus revealed himself as the source of the Living Water. This water can be used to dilute the strong alcoholic drink so those in the village would come to their senses and recognize Jesus as he is.

When Jesus spoke to her, she was surprised, because Jews did not speak to Samaritans. In fact, she asked Jesus why a Jew would speak to a Samaritan. She stressed their difference. For Jesus, that did not matter. Jesus came and spoke with an enemy. In fact, Jesus showed his vulnerability by asking her for water - the basic requirement for life!

What happened is quite interesting. As Jesus and the woman talked, Jesus slowly revealed himself to her. At first, she resisted and was antagonistic. She talked about her race. Then she asked Jesus if he was greater than her ancestor, Jacob.

When we enter into a conversation with Jesus, it is always an opportunity for him to reveal himself. It is also an opportunity for us to remove whatever hinders us from knowing him. Jesus saw the woman was tired from fetching water. So he spoke to her in a way she would want what he had to offer.

The woman wondered how Jesus was going to give her Living Water when he had nothing with him to draw water from the well. But Jesus is God. He is the source of the Living Water. This water is for everyone. Everyone can get this. All one has to do is ask Jesus for it.

> *Lord, you are the source of the Living Water. I thirst for you because without you, I cannot live. You are my life. I want to know you more. Jesus, give me this Living Water to refresh me.*

RECEIVING THE LIVING WATER

When the Samaritan woman asked Jesus for the Living Water, she probably did not know what she was asking. She asked for water from the superficial perspective. But Jesus meant it from a deeper spiritual perspective. For Jesus, that did not matter. Her response was enough. Jesus gave the Living Water to her just because she asked for it. He immediately asked her to bring her husband to him.

It turned out the woman had five husbands and the man she was with was not her husband. Jesus made her confront her sinfulness. This was how he gave her the Living Water. By doing so, the woman got to know Jesus. She became convinced Jesus was the Messiah. The woman repented and came to Jesus.

Similarly, we receive the Living Water when we confront our sinfulness; look at sin in the eye, name it and confess it to others so we will have power over it. Once this is done, Jesus can release the Water of Life to us. Without repentance, we cannot have a new life.

> *Lord, let me confront my sins. May I see them as they really are - things that separate me from you. Lord, wash away my iniquity and cleanse me from my sins.*

TRUE WORSHIP

After setting up his Church where he will be worshiped, Jesus spoke of worship in spirit and truth. Worship does not depend on a place. It is our disposition when we come before God. It is knowing where we stand before God. This knowledge and awareness of our position before God will lead us to do the will of God.

> *Jesus, may I worship you in Spirit and in truth. Let me know you and let me know where I stand before you. You are my God. I am your child, the one you love. Let me know that you alone can give me life. Let me come to you O Lord.*

True worship leads to true knowledge of Jesus. The woman got to know Jesus as the Messiah. Receiving the Living Water is worshiping in Spirit and truth.

Jesus gave the woman the Living Water. Now, it started to spring up from her, leading to eternal life. This spring of water overflowed from her and led her to go back to town and proclaim Jesus to others. The water that started at the well now becomes a flood; all because the woman received the Living Water. The water from the well was forgotten because she did not need it. She had the Living Water flowing from her.

One thing to note about the woman is when she went back to town, she said about Jesus, *"He told me everything that I did."* However, if one looks at her conversation with Jesus, the only time Jesus spoke about her personal life was when he asked her to bring her husband. Most of the time, Jesus spoke about giving her the Living Water. Her whole life revolved around her broken relationships.

This woman was probably searching for something in her life. Her life was full of misery and pain. She was missing something in her life and she found it when she found Jesus.

Many people look for God in many ways. Some of them are like this woman, searching for God in relationships with people - only to learn these cannot satisfy. Only Jesus can satisfy one's heart.

When she received the Living Water, she knew she had found what she was looking for. She left with joy.

This water was dropped into the strong alcoholic drink and now, the town was not drunk anymore. The water diluted the wine so people could enjoy it. By giving the Living Water to the woman, Jesus proved to her - he was greater than her ancestor, Jacob.

Jacob gave her village the water from the well. Jesus gave her the Living Water. He was the fulfillment of Israel.

> *Jesus, give me this Living Water so I will not have to draw water from other sources. Lord, may this water fill me and overflow to others.*

Speak about Jesus

The woman went off and told the town about Jesus and what he did for her. She said, *"Come, see a man who told me everything that I did. Can this be the Christ?"* She invited people to Jesus. She spoke about Jesus and she told them what he did. She did not talk about rituals or Laws or rules. This proclamation of the gospel is everyone's duty. What is needed is to proclaim Jesus as he is and to tell people of what he has done to us personally.

She ended her statement with a question: *"Can this be the Christ?"* I have to answer these questions: Who is Jesus to me? Is he MY Christ? Proclaiming the gospel requires an invitation to look deeper into one's relationship with Jesus. Who is Jesus to you?

When she proclaimed Jesus, many people believed her. Jesus stayed with them for two days. After those two days, they believed because they heard his word. Now, it was not the experience of others that mattered to them. What mattered was their relationship with Jesus. They believed because they knew him.

> *Lord, may I have courage to preach you as you are. Lead me to you. Guide me to you O God. Reveal yourself to me Lord Jesus, and give me courage to speak about you, about who you are to me. Give me the wisdom to let others look into their relationship with you. Let them also seek you and know you are THEIR Christ and Savior.*

The Source of Living Water Heals

The second part of this chapter shows a nobleman coming to Jesus because his son was close to death. This miracle happened at the same place where Jesus changed the water to wine.

The nobleman lived in the Old Covenant. The Law was powerless to save his child. By coming to Jesus, he admitted the saving power of Jesus. The water of the Old Covenant was changed to the wine of the New Covenant.

By leaving when Jesus told him, he believed and received what he asked for.

> *Jesus, you have the power to save. Remove my old self. Instead, give me new water to renew me. I want you Lord and I need you. Come to my life Lord.*

Chapter 5

Jesus: Equal to the Father

Jesus came to a gate at the Temple. The gate was called
Sheep gate. At the gate was a pool called Bethesda, which
means *"house of kindness."* A lot of people were at the
gate. The people were at the Sheep gate - like sheep
without a shepherd.

HEALING OF THE LAME MAN

Jesus saw a lame man and spoke to him. The man and the
others who were sick were waiting for an angel to stir the
water. The first one to jump into the pool would be healed.
People were focused on the water to stir, yet, the source of
Living Water was in their midst and they did not recognize
him.

How often have I looked at things to find Jesus? How
often have things blinded me from seeing Jesus right in
front of me?

> *Lord, let me see you when you are before me. Let me
> know and recognize you O Lord.*

With the healing, Jesus showed he was the source of the
Living Water who heals. There was no need to wait for an
angel to stir the water because the Son of God, God
himself, was here. Jesus also asked the man if he wanted
to be healed. Jesus had to ask this question because there
are some who prefer to live in their misery than to come to
ask Jesus for healing.

Instead of answering Jesus, the man told Jesus about his
condition and how he could not be healed. He spoke of the

miraculous manner where healing would take place. The water had to move, it had to come to life, before healing can take place.

The man said, *"Sir, I have no one to put me into the pool."* The man wondered how he could be healed when he needed someone to put him into the pool. With Jesus, there was no need for any one's help. Jesus himself is our help. By his word, God created the universe. By a word, he can create a new person. With a word, Jesus healed the man.

The man did not have to wait for the water to come to life because he was before the source of the Living Water himself.

The healing brought controversy because it happened on a Sabbath. The man broke the Law. By carrying his mat, he worked on the Sabbath. The leaders saw the broken Law, but Jesus saw the broken man. For Jesus, the man was more important than the Law. The Sabbath was made for man.

The man did not know Jesus at that time. But Jesus revealed himself to the man who told the leaders. For the leaders, Jesus broke the Law because he healed on the Sabbath. Because of this, they planned to kill him. The Law clearly stated that anyone who broke the Sabbath was to be stoned to death. Jesus broke the Law - so he had to die.

THE FATHER AND JESUS

When confronted by the leaders, Jesus had an interesting conversation with them. Jesus made himself equal to God. He called God his Father. Although Jesus and the Father are different persons, they are still one God with the Holy Spirit. This is a mystery that cannot be explained.

Jesus said, "*My Father is still working, so I am working, too.*" When Jesus said this, he was putting himself equal to God. To the leaders, Jesus was not only a breaker of the Sabbath, he was now also a blasphemer. Because of this, the leaders persecuted him.

The Father gave Jesus authority over all creation so Jesus is Lord of the Sabbath. The Father showed Jesus the things he did and Jesus followed the Father. The Father will show even greater things so people may marvel.

> *Lord Jesus, I want to see the great things the Father will do through you. Open my eyes O God so I may see the marvels you will do and are doing for me!*

JESUS GIVES LIFE

Life comes from the Father. He gives life. Since Jesus is God, he also gives life to whoever he wants. The purpose of this is for people to honor the Father. Jesus has authority over all things - including death. The dead will rise when they hear his voice. This authority comes from the Father. The Father is honored when Jesus is honored. Jesus came to honor the Father.

When we hear the voice of Jesus and believe in the Father, we pass on to life. The dead will rise just by hearing the voice of Jesus. Jesus also spoke of his second coming when everyone in the tomb would hear his voice and would rise for judgment.

Whenever someone sins, that person breaks their relationship with God. In the case of mortal sins, they made a decision to separate themselves totally from God. Their soul dies due to the mortal sin.

With repentance as celebrated in the sacrament of confession, the repentant heart and the words of absolution from the priest restore the person back to life. The priest speaks the words of Jesus. By those words, the priest spiritually raises the dead from the tomb.

> *Lord, your sacrament is a wonderful gift. It brings me back to life. It restores to me the dignity you have planned for me even before the creation of the world. I thank you for giving me this sacrament. Through the words of the priest, I have new life. Thank you also for priests who minister to your people.*

BELIEVE IN JESUS

Jesus then pointed to the testimony of John the Baptist. He also pointed to the testimony of the Father. What Jesus said is true. His works proved this. His Father proved this. John the Baptist proved this. All of them testified that Jesus came from the Father.

Scripture points to Jesus. To believe in scripture is to believe in Jesus. To believe this, one has to seek glory from the Father. If one seeks glory from other people, one will not know Jesus. The key is to honor the Father.

To have the word of Jesus living in me, I must believe in him first. Only then can these words have meaning. No matter how much time I spend in searching scripture, if I do not believe in Jesus, I will not have eternal life.

The leaders searched scriptures thinking these bring eternal life. But here, Life himself was before them. Scriptures pointed to Jesus, yet they did not want to believe.

Jesus gave the reason why they did not want to believe in him - they were more concerned with the praise from men.

> *Lord, I want to believe you. May I seek your praise rather than men's. May I believe you through the testimony of the Father and through Scripture. Open my eyes so I may believe. Give me courage so I may seek only to please you.*

Chapter 6

The Father's Will

This chapter begins with a multitude following Jesus. They followed for the wrong reasons. Even so, Jesus was still concerned about them. He asked Philip a question to *test* him.

Very often I hear people say God is testing them to see how strong their faith is. I personally do not believe this. In saying so, one is saying God does not know one's heart.

Scripture clearly tells us God knows our hearts. If Jesus knew the hearts of men, he certainly knew the heart and faith of Philip. Jesus did not have to see how strong his faith was.

The word used here in the original Greek was used four times in scripture. It was first used to describe Satan as the Tempter. This was also used to describe a lawyer coming to *test* Jesus. It is used here in this verse, where Jesus *tests* Philip. And lastly, St. Paul used this to describe the Tempter *testing* us.

Looking at the context of how the word was used, we get a sense of what this word means. In the case of the Tempter, he wanted Jesus to change the stones to bread. The Tempter wanted Jesus to act in a way that would lead him to fall. In the case of the lawyer, he was also leading Jesus to say what he wanted to hear.

In this case, Jesus was *testing* Philip to lead Philip to do what he wanted Philip to do. So, this *testing* is not to see how strong Philip's faith was. Jesus was teaching Philip a lesson in trusting God. The next verse proves this by saying Jesus *"himself knew what he would do."*

What Philip saw was a lot of people. What Jesus saw was the lack of food. Jesus did not tell the people to leave. Instead, he multiplied the food.

> *Lord, may I see your hand when you 'test' me. May I respond in trust. Lead me to a deeper understanding of who you really are.*

GIVE EVERYTHING TO JESUS

The sign happened, not only because of Jesus. It happened because someone cooperated with him. God performs signs with the cooperation of people. The sign started with a boy giving Jesus the five loaves and two fish. From there, Jesus passed the food to his disciples.

The multitude wanted to see the signs but not believe. The important thing is to believe in Jesus - if not for his words, then for his works. Jesus is able to take what we have and multiply it. What matters is not the quantity we give but what we give and how we give. We give all in trust.

> *Lord, may I give you my all, in trust. Take Lord and receive. Use them all for your glory.*

JESUS IS

The crowd wanted to make Jesus king, but he withdrew to the mountain by himself. The people wanted to mold him into their image, but Jesus knew what the Father wanted. The only thing Jesus wanted was to do the Father's will. No one can dictate to God. Jesus is God so he does things his way.

The disciples left without Jesus and went to the other side of the lake by boat. They were going against strong wind.

Jesus came to them walking on the water and they did not recognize him. They were afraid. They took him in only after he called to them and identified himself and they immediately reached their destination.

When he called to the disciples, he said, "*It is I. Don't be afraid.*" The words translated as "*It is I*" literally is "*I AM*". God revealed himself to Moses as the I AM. With this, Jesus revealed himself as God.

When Jesus comes, we will not recognize him and will even be afraid. We will recognize Jesus only when he calls to us. In our difficulties and storms in life, Jesus will reveal himself as the I AM.

> *In my life Lord, there will be storms. I will struggle against these on my own and still not be able to conquer them. When you come, I will be scared because I will not see this as your hand. Yet, if I trust and accept you, let you into my situation, you will lead me to where I need to go. My courage comes from faith that Jesus is God. When I believe Jesus is God, then everything falls into place. Let me hear you tell me you are God!*

BREAD FROM HEAVEN

People looked for Jesus because they wanted something from him. They did not come to him because they believed. Jesus knew this. He told them not to work for what can perish. According to him, "*this is doing God's work: to believe in the one whom he sent.*"

Many people mistakenly think good works will save them. The Pharisees were ritually pure. They were blameless. Yet, according to Jesus, this was not enough. They were not doing God's work. According to Jesus, doing God's work is believing in the one whom the Father sent - Jesus himself.

Jesus leads to eternal life because he gives food that lasts. Jesus is the bread out of heaven. Come to Jesus and not be hungry. Believe and not be thirsty.

The people asked Jesus for a sign - one similar to what Moses did - where he gave them manna in the desert. Jesus said, *"Most certainly, I tell you, it wasn't Moses who gave you the bread out of heaven, but my Father gives you the true bread out of heaven."* Notice the tenses in the words.

Jesus said, *"it wasn't Moses who gave you bread."* This happened in the past. Then he said, *"My Father gives you the true bread out of heaven"* - in the present tense. The food their ancestors ate in the desert stopped when they entered the Promised Land. But God continues to bless us every day by giving us the bread from heaven. God's blessings never end because his love never ends.

The people then asked him, *"Lord, always give us this bread."* The tone from the people changed. At first, they called Jesus *"Rabbi"*. Now, they called him *"Lord"*. From there, Jesus started to give them the bread from heaven.

He revealed himself. *"He who comes to me will never be hungry, he who believes in me will never be thirsty."*

We shall be satisfied only if we come to Jesus, approach him in humility and trust.

> *Jesus my God, I will trust in you. I need to trust in you because you are my only hope. I can trust no one else but you. Only by trusting in you can I have the life of the Father. Living in obedience is the key to living your life.*

Jesus will not lose those the Father gives. Jesus will not throw away those who come to him. In the midst of trouble and hardship, Jesus is ALWAYS there!

Understanding Jesus is a gift from the Father. The Father draws people. Without this, we will not know Jesus. However, we also need to respond through repentance. I must listen to Jesus. When I listen to Jesus, the Father will raise me up.

Jesus revealed himself as the Bread of Life. He started giving the Living Bread. When Jesus reveals himself, he gives himself.

EAT THE FLESH

The Father gives us Jesus. He gives us his flesh. Eating the flesh of Jesus appears five times in this chapter. This is a critical point John wanted to make. We need to eat the flesh of Jesus to live. Manna gave life, but it did not give eternal life. Now, the Son of God comes down from heaven and he gives eternal life. What does it mean to eat the flesh of Jesus?

"He who comes to me will not be hungry" - because he will eat the flesh of the Son of God. To eat the flesh of Jesus is to come to him. To come to him is to hear the voice of the Father and learn from him.

"He who believes in me will never be thirsty" - because he will drink the blood of the Son of God. To drink his blood is to believe in him.

When we come to receive the body and blood of Jesus in the Eucharist, we are not coming to receive bread and wine. As Catholics, we believe this is literally Jesus himself - his Body and Blood, Soul and Divinity! We come so Jesus can feed us. We come because we heard the Father's word and had learned from him. We come because we believe in Jesus!

God gives the grace, people respond. Many of his disciples left because they did not understand. They did not respond to God's revelation. One interesting thought is Jesus did not call them back nor did he change his teachings. Which means one thing: what he taught was and still is true. There is no compromise to the teachings of Jesus.

It is quite sad to see communities compromise the truth in the interest of attracting more people. Sadly, these communities die rather than thrive.

For the Twelve, they stayed even if they did not understand. What they knew was Jesus spoke the words of eternal life. Faith is not a matter of understanding. It is a matter of believing the person because we know he speaks the truth.

This does not mean we should not use our minds. Our human capability can only take us so far in understanding Jesus. There has to be a decision to believe and trust in Jesus - even if one does not understand what he says.

Lord, indeed, your teachings are hard to accept. Yet, you have the words of eternal life. To whom should I go? Even if I do not understand, even if what you tell me is hard, I will believe because this is true life. I will obey you because it unlocks your power. This is the only way to see you my God.

Chapter 7

Who is Jesus?

This chapter mentions the brothers of Jesus. Catholics believe Mary remained a virgin even after giving birth to Jesus. Based on this belief, the *brothers* of Jesus in scripture mean cousins or relatives. One can go into debates about this, but this book is not the venue for such discussion.

Any time is the right time for those who are not in Jesus. Jesus works in his way and in his own time. He is never late. This right time also depends on the Father's timing. Jesus told his brothers it was not yet time. Even his brothers did not believe him and even his brothers were not able to sway him. Jesus is God.

For times when Jesus seems absent, he is still there. Believe that Jesus is always there but is unrecognized, waiting for the right time.

> *Lord, you promised to be with us. In times when I do not see you, when you seem absent, when things do not make sense, Lord, teach me to trust in you. Let me believe you will intervene at the right time.*

The leaders were looking for Jesus. The multitude could not agree about him. Yet, despite all these discussions, John wrote, *"No one spoke openly about him."* Everyone kept their own opinions about Jesus to themselves.

At the right time, Jesus went up and taught. People were amazed at what he knew because he had no formal education.

KNOWING THE FATHER

Jesus learned from his Father and repeated what the Father said. Jesus said, *"If anyone wants to do the will of the Father, he will know about the teaching whether it is from God or from myself."* There are a lot of ideas about Jesus. But which ones are true?

One must be discerning in what one hears. To discern what is being taught, to see whether it is from God or not, one must have the sincere desire to know the truth.

To know whether one is righteous or not, one must see whose glory that person is seeking. If that person seeks God's glory, then he will stay true. If he seeks his own glory, then that person will not stay true. Jesus seeks the glory of the Father - the one who sent him. Jesus is true because he is the Truth.

Preachers should seek the glory of the Father. Otherwise, Jesus will accuse them and challenge their beliefs and assumptions. The leaders wanted to kill Jesus. Similarly, those who seek their own glory seek to stifle the message of Jesus. They will twist the truth to please other people. But Jesus will have none of that. He challenges people of their beliefs when they are wrong.

> *Lord, let me seek your glory. Let me desire only YOUR glory. May I seek to please you and not anyone else. Let me speak YOUR words. Let me speak YOUR truth.*

BELIEVING IN JESUS

To believe in Jesus is to be open to his leading. This will allow one to see things through God's eyes and judge by what is right.

Jesus was sent by the Father. He said, *"I know him, because I am from him and he sent me."* Because of this claim, people wanted to take him. But again, he escaped because it was not his time. Jesus was in control. The leaders could not take hold of him. The multitude believed in him because of the signs he performed. The leaders saw this and they plotted to arrest him.

Jesus already prophesied he would be leaving. Where he was going, no one could follow. The reason for this is because he is the only one who can redeem the world.

"You will seek me and not find me." When Jesus seems absent, he is actually redeeming us. Only he can do this. We will search for him at that time and not find him.

"If anyone is thirsty, let him come to me and drink! He who believes in me, as the Scripture has said, from within him will flow rivers of living water." To come to Jesus is to believe in him. When we believe in Jesus, rivers of Living Water will flow from us. This is the Holy Spirit as was shown in Chapter 4 with the Samaritan woman.

The multitude believed in Jesus, but the leaders did not. They knew their scripture, and although the fulfillment of scripture was before them they could not recognize it. They continued to cling to their idea of who the Messiah was so when Jesus confronted them, they could not see. The people believed because of what they heard.

> *Lord, teach me to believe in you. I come to you to drink the waters of eternal life. Lord, challenge me of my beliefs. Lead me to the right path.*

Chapter 8

Slavery and Freedom

This chapter begins with Jesus, the Light of the World,
sitting down and teaching the crowd early in the morning.
The Pharisees brought a woman and accused her of
adultery. They wanted to stone her according to the Law.
In response, Jesus wrote on the ground. What he wrote is
not known. There was only one instance where scripture
showed God's finger writing something: when he gave the
Law to Moses.

Since the Pharisees were questioning him about the Law, it
is possible the author wanted to show God writing the
perfect Law. This Law is the Law of mercy and love,
rather than the Law of fear.

> *Lord, reveal to me the perfect Law - the Law of mercy
> and love.*

God's Mercy

When they came to him, the leaders were arrogant and
self-righteous. But Jesus revealed to them the truth and
they were *"convicted by their conscience"*. They slowly
left until there was only Jesus and the woman.

At the start, Jesus was sitting with his disciples when the
scribes and Pharisees brought the woman to him. Now he
stood up, saw her and talked to her. When Jesus stood, he
assumed the posture of a king ready to pass judgment. But
instead of judgment, the woman received mercy. Her
dignity was restored by the mercy of God.

God defends us and pours out his mercy and love. St. Paul says, *"There is therefore now no condemnation to those who are in Christ Jesus."* For those who trust in Jesus, those who strive to live in union with him, there is no condemnation. Our past sins are forgiven and we are restored to our dignity. Such is the mercy of God.

> *Lord, as far as the east is from the west, you have thrown away my sins. Such is the greatness of your mercy. Let me be mercy to others in my life.*

LIGHT OF THE WORLD

When the woman left, Jesus spoke to the crowd. Some Pharisees were still in the crowd. *"I am the Light of the world. He who follows me will not walk in the darkness, but will have the light of life."* This was too much for the Pharisees.

Jesus spoke the truth and they would not accept it. Even when his accusers confronted him, Jesus would not take back what he said. The Father was with him. Jesus knew he had the truth so he left judgment to the Father. The important thing for Jesus was the presence of his Father. Nothing else mattered.

Jesus was not lying. He does not lie because he spoke only what the Father wanted him to say.

> *Father, let me hold on to you. Let me cling to you because I find life only in you. Lord Jesus, teach me to hold on to the Father. Teach me to obey him. Only in doing so can I come to know him.*

REPENTANCE: RESPONDING TO GOD

The Pharisees now asked Jesus who his Father was. Jesus said they had to know him first before they could know his

Father. Jesus then said, *"I am going away, and you will seek me, and you will die in your sins."*

For those who do not believe, even if they want to, they cannot find Jesus. It is interesting when they asked Jesus, they did not ask about dying in their sins. They were more concerned about where Jesus was going.

For them, they had no sin. They could not understand Jesus because they could not accept they had sinned. They refused to repent and so, could not understand him.

Jesus continued, *"unless you believe that I am he, you will die in your sins."* The phrase, *"I am he"* is literally written as *"I AM"*. So, another way to read this is, *"unless you believe that I AM, you will die in your sins."* To know Jesus, one has to believe he is God. Without this belief, everything Jesus says will mean nothing.

SLAVES TO SIN

They continued to ask Jesus who he was. Jesus took them back to the beginning.

God had been revealing himself from the beginning. The only question is whether we are willing to respond to him. Those who do not respond to God's revelation are still in sin. They are still slaves to sin.

When Jesus is lifted up, then people will know him. The crucifixion of Jesus is the fulfillment of God's revelation. Symbolically, if we lift Jesus up, put him above ourselves, humble ourselves, we will be able to know who he is.

Accept the truth and it will set you free. The Pharisees did not want to accept the truth - that is why they lived in their sin. They were still slaves of their preconceived ideas.

> *Lord, teach me to accept the truth. Teach me to get rid of my preconceived ideas about you. Teach me O Lord, to raise you up, to accept you as you are so I may see and know myself.*

KNOWING THE TRUTH

Jesus spoke the truth, but many did not believe him. People wanted to kill him because he spoke the truth. Truth cannot be killed. The messenger might be killed, but truth will always find a way to get through.

The leaders first claimed Abraham as their father. Then they claimed God as their father. Jesus refuted that. He said Abraham believed and rejoiced when he saw that day.

To be a child of God, one has to understand Jesus. Understanding comes from hearing the word of God. The reason why one does not hear is because one is not of God. This is a choice one has to make: do I want to belong to God or not?

Sit down in silence and listen to Jesus. Believe in him and you will know the truth. The woman caught in adultery remained silent before Jesus. She trusted in his mercy.

Those enslaved to sin are those who refuse to accept Jesus. A repentant sinner is one who continues to work for his freedom. The slave is one who is complacent and therefore, arrogant of his faith. This person is not willing to change his view. That is the slave.

Knowing and listening to the truth is a choice. One can choose to listen or one can choose to reject it.

> *Lord, I choose to listen to you. I want to know the truth so I can be set free. Lord God, help me. Guide me and teach me. Strip away my arrogance so I may see you and accept you at your word.*

48

Chapter 9

New Eyes to See Jesus

The chapter begins with Jesus and his disciples seeing a man born blind. During the time of Jesus, sickness was believed to be caused by sin. Jesus corrected this and said sickness and suffering have their purpose: to show God's work. Jesus then spat on the ground and made mud, put the mud on the man's eyes and told him to wash at the pool called Siloam which meant "*Sent*". The man did as Jesus said and he was healed.

The man had been sick since birth. He had probably been praying for sight ever since he was able to pray. His parents said he was of age. He was already an adult - so at least 20 years old. For him, healing did come after all these years.

We too need healing. When we pray, we too will be healed. From our perspective it may delay, but it will surely come. God is never late.

> *Lord, heal me of my sickness and sinfulness. Heal me Jesus. I was born a sinner - have mercy O God and heal me.*

Seeing God

Jesus came to show the works of the Father. Jesus made mud and rubbed it on the man's eyes. God made man from the ground. By doing this, Jesus was making new eyes for the man born blind. Now he will be given new eyes so he can see Jesus clearly.

Similarly, we also are blind to several things. We cannot see what God has planned for us. We cannot even see God for who he is. We need to see God through new eyes. We cannot see God through the same set of eyes. We need to get rid of preconceived ideas of who he is and see him through new eyes. Only Jesus can give these new eyes.

> *Lord, give me new eyes to see you as you are.*

TESTIFYING FOR JESUS

This chapter shows how the blind man slowly got to know who Jesus was. He was able to do so not by following him, but by answering the questions asked of him. First, his neighbors asked him and he said, *"The man called Jesus."*

His neighbors brought him to the Pharisees. They also asked him how he was healed. His first response was *"He is a prophet."*

The Pharisees then asked him under oath to tell them how he was healed. When they commanded him to *"Give glory to God"*, it was a command to speak the truth under oath. The man obeyed his leaders. He gave glory to God by speaking of his healing and Jesus. Healing is personal. Only we can speak of it. Healing is also to be proclaimed because this is God's work.

> *Jesus, give me the courage to speak about you, of the healing I received from you. O God, give glory to your name through a sinner like me.*

JESUS IS GOD

The man asked them *"Do you want to be his disciples?"* Now, the man saw Jesus as a teacher. The Pharisees responded they did not know where Jesus came from. With this, they were saying Jesus was a nobody. It can also be an insult, meaning they could not trace his ancestry - therefore, he had no human father. As such, he was someone born out of sin.

By saying they did not know where Jesus came from, they were right also. Jesus, in fact, had no human father. Jesus was God and Jesus IS God!

The man continued to argue with the Pharisees and told them Jesus was not a sinner. Instead, Jesus was one who does the will of God. The man proceeded, to take the conversation to the beginning. *"Since the world began, no one has opened the eyes of a blind man."* And he concluded Jesus was someone from God. By bringing the discussion to the beginning, the man was getting closer to knowing who Jesus was. Jesus was with God from the beginning, so he is God!

Because of this, the Pharisees condemned both the man and Jesus as sinners and they threw the man out of the community.

Here we see the Pharisees and the man saying the same things. One was saying it to condemn and insult Jesus. The other was saying it to give glory to God. This is also a warning to us. Just because someone speaks the right words, does not mean they are preaching Jesus. For all we know, they might be against Jesus.

FACE TO FACE WITH JESUS

The blind man also showed progress in his knowledge of Jesus. He first called Jesus a man. Then he said Jesus was a prophet, then a teacher, then someone who was from God then someone from the beginning. There was gradual progression in his knowledge of Jesus. The man's knowledge of Jesus deepened, not because of his constant contact with Jesus, but because he spoke about his experience with Jesus. This is evangelization - to speak about what God has done for us.

As he spoke about Jesus, everything that mattered to him was slowly taken away. His neighbors left him. His parents left him on his own. His community threw him out. Lastly, he was denied worship of his God. He was all alone. Then, Jesus came to him face to face.

Similarly for us, in the midst of our despair, in the midst of our problems, in the midst of our difficulties - when everything we hold dear is taken away - we come face to face with Jesus and we hear the same question Jesus asked the blind man: *"Do you believe in the Son of God?"* Notice Jesus addressed himself as *"Son of God"* rather than Son of Man.

The blind man answered, *"Who is he Lord, that I may believe in him."* At this point in his knowledge of Jesus, he called Jesus *"Lord"*. Jesus told him, *"You have both seen him and it is he who speaks to you."* He said, *"Lord, I believe!"* and he worshiped him. Noticed the word used, *"worship"*. Worship is reserved only for God.

The man got so far to knowing Jesus. He stopped short of calling Jesus as God. Jesus had to reveal himself before the man finally saw who Jesus was.

Knowing Jesus is a grace. It is God's gift. This happens when we come face to face with Jesus. When we see Jesus, we should believe him and worship him.

> *Lord, the result of knowing you is detachment from other things. The blind man lost everything but he came to know you. When confronted with loss O Lord, let me remember you are before me - face to face, revealing yourself to me. May I respond to you O God and worship you for who you are!*

Spiritual Blindness

The leaders could not believe because they were enslaved by their own ideas. They could not accept Jesus as the Messiah. To make it worse, they claimed they knew what they were doing. Because of this, there was no repentance; therefore, they remained in their sin.

But the man who was healed knew who Jesus was because he experienced the healing of Jesus. Even with people persecuting him, he continued to proclaim his healing. He proclaimed who Jesus was - the one who healed him - a prophet, a good man, a man from God, someone from the beginning. And when he was thrown out of the synagogue, denying him forever of his God, he came face to face with God himself! He believed and he worshiped.

With new eyes, we see Jesus.

> *Jesus, give me new eyes. Heal my blindness so I can see you and worship you.*

This chapter ends with the leaders saying they were not blind. Jesus told them since they said they see, then their sin remained.

Spiritual blindness is caused by pride which is a failure to admit one's faults. The leaders claimed they see. They would not admit their mistakes. By saying this, they claimed they knew the truth.

From Jesus' perspective, since they knew the truth, and they still would not admit their mistake, then they remained in their sinfulness. Their pride prevented them from admitting their sinfulness.

> *Lord, break through my pride. I am blind. Let me see my faults so I can truly see you.*

Chapter 10

Abundant Life in Jesus

As the leaders claimed they were not blind and Jesus accused them of remaining in their sin, Jesus talked about shepherds. There seems to be two parts in this discussion. In the first part, Jesus spoke of himself as the gate to the sheepfold. He was talking about shepherds who go through the door and thieves who climb the fence.

Those who go through Jesus are true shepherds. They wait for Jesus to open the gate before they enter. They wait for the right opportunity before they go in and call the sheep.

The thief does not wait. He goes in forcibly to steal, kill, and destroy. The true shepherd waits for the gate to open before calling his sheep by name and leading them out.

Jesus: The Gate

Jesus is the gate that protects the sheep against wild animals and those with bad intentions. Thieves will come to mislead the sheep. The sheep will not willingly listen to the thief. They have the desire to follow the shepherd, but the thief will attempt to steal, kill and destroy.

Jesus said he will not lose those whom the Father has given him. The sheep will not be lost. They will not follow the thief. In fact, they will run away. But that does not prevent the thief from attacking them. The sheep should take shelter in the gate because Jesus came to give life to the sheep. Those who enter by him will be safe. They will go in and go out and find pasture.

The thief is the devil. He comes to steal, to kill and to destroy. He will deceive and take the sheep by force by attacking them. But Jesus is the gate. He protects his sheep and gives them life - a superabundant life.

> *Lord, help me discern your voice. Let me not be misled by other voices. I want to hear your voice alone. Lead me to the life you have planned for me.*

JESUS: THE GOOD SHEPHERD

In the second part, Jesus said, "*I am the good shepherd.*" The Good Shepherd gives his life for his sheep. The hired hand looks after his own interest only. The Pharisees were not looking after their sheep. They were corrupt and wanted to get only what they could. They were not willing to stay and fight, but they left at the first sign of trouble.

Whereas the devil is aggressive and active, the hired hand just does not care. He does things because it is expected. He does these, not because it is the right thing to do, but because he gets something out of it.

Jesus contrasts himself to the hired-hand. Jesus is concerned about his sheep. He knows them and he willingly lays down his life for his sheep. When the wolf comes, he fights the wolf and defends his flock. More importantly, he knows his own and they know him; just as the Father knows Jesus and Jesus knows the Father.

For Jesus to know his sheep is understandable since God knows our hearts. But for the sheep to know Jesus as well as the Father knows Jesus - this is impossible on our own. Yet this is God's plan. God has given us the grace to know Jesus. We just need to respond.

> *Lord, may I respond to your grace so I may know you as intimately as the Father knows you.*

Jesus gave his life, not only to those he has in the sheepfold, but in other sheepfolds. Those in the sheepfold are the Jews, while those outside are the Gentiles. It is God's will to unite everyone under one Shepherd - Jesus. Jesus died for everyone.

By saying he was the Good Shepherd, Jesus implied he was God. Psalm 95:7 says, *"for he is our God. We are the people of his pasture, and the sheep in his care. Today, oh that you would hear his voice!"*

Many people argued about Jesus again. Some said he was possessed and insane. Others said he was not and proposed he could be the one they were waiting for.

> *Lord, let me hear your voice. Call me Lord. May I respond when you call me.*

THE SHEEP HEAR HIS VOICE

The Feast of Dedication is mentioned in this chapter. This feast is also called the Feast of Lights. It commemorates the time when the second temple was rededicated after it was defiled during the Greek occupation of Jerusalem. During the rededication, there was enough oil to light the lamps for one day. Miraculously, the oil burned until the eighth day.

The author also said this happened in winter and Jesus was walking in the temple in Solomon's porch. Solomon's porch was said to be the remnant of the first temple. Here, John was showing the three temples in one place - the first temple built by Solomon, the second temple built after the return from the exile, and the last Temple, Jesus himself. The leaders came to Jesus and asked him to tell them plainly if he was the Christ.

Jesus always answers these questions.

He had been revealing himself plainly but they would not believe. So he asked them to look at his works. He said the reason they did not believe was because they were not his sheep. His sheep hear his voice and follow him. The reason why no one can snatch them from Jesus is because he is the Son of God - co-equal to the Father.

The leaders were scandalized by what Jesus said. They asked Jesus to reveal himself and when he did, they could not take what he said. They wanted to kill him.

Similarly, when we ask Jesus to reveal himself, we will be amazed at what he will show. It is far beyond our comprehension.

The leaders wanted to seize Jesus but he went out of their hands. Being the Son of God, he was able to go through their hands even if they wanted to kill him. Jesus was in control.

You may be facing overwhelming difficulties now. One thing this incident shows is Jesus can go through any danger. If we follow Jesus, we too will be able to go through these difficulties and dangers. These will not go away. With Jesus we will walk victoriously through all these.

> *Lord, let me accept you as you are. Let me accept what you say to me - even if it is too amazing for me to believe. Lord God, help me to know you. I want to know you. Let me not be scandalized when what you say does not agree with what I believe. Instead, let me believe you because you are the Lord my God.*

Chapter 11

The Resurrection

The chapter begins with the mention of Lazarus, Mary and Martha. Mary was also mentioned as the one who anointed Jesus with oil and wiped his feet with her hair. The sisters sent a messenger to Jesus and asked him to come. The way they phrased the request is interesting: *"Lord, behold, he for whom you have great affection is sick."*

Having heard this, Jesus said this sickness would not end in death. This would show the glory of God. This would also glorify the Son of God. The verse also said Jesus loved the three siblings and when he heard of the news, he remained for two more days.

If someone was dying, the first reaction of someone who loves the dying is to rush to the person's death bed. But Jesus did the opposite. He stayed for two more days.

Jesus allows sickness and death for the glory of God.

Mary and Martha tried to force the hand of God - they tried to manipulate Jesus to come to them. Yet, Jesus, being God, knew what he was doing. He was still in control. It was precisely his love of the three that made him stay for two more days, to show them the power and glory of God.

God allows difficulties to come, not as punishment, but to show us his power and glory. He allows death, our death to sin, so we can see his glory. God wants to show his children the power of their Father.

> *Lord, when I do not understand the events in my life,*
> *let me know you are in control. Teach me to know you*
> *are there and my future is in your hands. How often*
> *Lord, have I tried to force your hand to do what I*
> *want. But Lord, teach me you are God. Let it be done*
> *to me according to your word.*

WALKING IN THE LIGHT

After two days, Jesus invited his disciples to go back to Judea. The disciples asked why he would want to go back to Jerusalem when the leaders wanted to kill him. Jesus told them about walking while there is light and stumbling when the light has gone. How was this related to their question? He spoke of a man walking in the light because he sees the light of the world, and stumbling in the night because the light is not in him.

This is about discernment. When we see Jesus, we walk with him - even if it leads to death. Jesus is in control and we follow as long as we see him. But when the light is not in me, I should stop and not proceed because certainly, I will stumble. We go where Jesus goes. Even if it is fearful, we go because we walk where there is light - we walk where the Light leads us.

After this, Jesus told them Lazarus was asleep. The disciples did not know he meant Lazarus was dead. Jesus told them plainly, *"Lazarus is dead."* Jesus compared Lazarus' death to sleep. For Jesus, death is a sleep. Lazarus was asleep but when the Light comes, the dead will wake up. The disciples followed Jesus, *"to die with him"*.

> *Jesus, help me see the Father's will. All I want is to do his will. Even if I do not know where you are leading, I must follow and I will follow. If through death, you are leading me to life. If through darkness, you are leading me to light. If through difficulties, you are leading me to victory. I may not understand, but I know you are the one I am following. In the end, it does not matter where I am going. What matters is who I am following. O Lord, how wonderful it is to follow you!*

Do You Believe?

When Jesus arrived, Lazarus had been dead for four days. Martha met Jesus outside the town. Martha blamed him for the death of her brother. She stopped short of asking Jesus to raise Lazarus. *"Even now I know that, whatever you ask of God, God will give you."* Jesus told her Lazarus would rise again.

Then came the revelation, *"I am the resurrection and the life. He who believes in me will still live, even if he dies. Whoever lives and believes in me will never die."* Then he asked a question, *"Do you believe this?"*

Notice what Jesus said. *"I am the resurrection."* Resurrection is a person and not only an event. It is SOMEONE to know - to experience.

The dead will rise and the living will not die. Jesus gives life! Jesus IS life! Everyone has to answer the question, *"Do you believe this?"*

Martha's response is interesting, *"Yes Lord, I do believe that you are the Christ, God's Son who comes into the world."* Martha probably did not understand nor know what Jesus meant, but she said *"Yes"* to Jesus. To Jesus, this was enough. Martha left immediately after professing her faith in Jesus. She went to call Mary, her sister.

> *Jesus, let me know you. I want to experience the*
> *resurrection in my life. Help me Lord, guide me. I*
> *want to believe that you give life, you are life! But*
> *Lord, through difficulties, often, I find it hard to*
> *believe. Remind me Jesus of your power to change*
> *my life. I want you so I can have this new life.*

MEETING JESUS

Jesus remained outside the city. Mary came to Jesus and she said the same words Martha said to Jesus. In our misery, Jesus meets us outside the bustle and noise. He stands outside until we approach him.

In her misery, Mary immediately fell down at Jesus' feet when she saw him. Jesus saw Mary and the Jews weeping and he groaned in his spirit. Why was Jesus troubled?

He knew Lazarus would rise from the dead. So he was not sad because of Lazarus' death. He groaned because he saw Mary and the Jews weeping. They were weeping because they had no hope. They mourned because Lazarus was dead and there was no more hope of seeing him.

But Jesus said he is the resurrection. He brings hope and he will give life where there is no hope. He gives life, where there is no life. People with no hope sadden Jesus. He wants people to trust in his mercy and power.

> *Lord, when there is no hope, let me turn to you. You*
> *are the only one who can save me. You are the only*
> *one who can give me hope. You are my hope!*
> *Trusting you is the only thing I can do. Take O Lord,*
> *everything I have for the glory of your name.*

Jesus wept when he saw the unbelief of Mary and the Jews. The Jews thought Jesus wept because of his love for Lazarus. True, Jesus loved Lazarus. But he did not weep because Lazarus was dead. He was going to raise Lazarus up in a few minutes, so why would he weep for his death?

John's gospel always has two meanings. The leaders were never right with regards to what Jesus thought. Jesus wept after Mary invited him to *"Come and see"* the tomb of Lazarus. He knew what was going to happen. He probably thought about the grief of the people. He probably wept because of the unbelief of the people.

In his revelation to St. Faustina, Jesus said he wants people to trust in him. I think this was why he wept. People had lost hope. They had no hope. They did not know who was before them, the one who could give life.

> *Lord, may I trust in you through difficulties. Come Lord and do as you wish. Jesus, I trust in you.*

SEEING THE GLORY OF GOD

When they came to the tomb, Jesus told them to remove the stone. Martha protested because according to her, the body was starting to decay. It was hopeless. But Jesus persisted, *"Didn't I tell you that if you believed, you would see God's glory?"*

Believe! Obey! Trust in Jesus and you will see the glory of God!

When Martha obeyed Jesus and had the stone removed, Jesus called to Lazarus, *"Lazarus, come out!"* And Lazarus did come out! Jesus did not give hope, because here, he fulfilled the hope. He gave life where there was no life.

In a hopeless situation, in a lifeless situation, in a desperate situation, Jesus takes it and turns it around by his power. God is powerful and by his word, he raised the dead. He can glorify our situation if we allow him.

> *Lord, in my situations, help me. Breathe life into them. No matter how desperate I may be, no matter how hopeless my situation, Jesus, I will trust in you.*

When Lazarus came out, his hands, feet and head were still bound. Jesus instructed the people, *"Free him, and let him go."* When Jesus raises us up, we need help from other people. We cannot live by ourselves. We cannot set ourselves free.

When Jesus saves us, he gives us life. But the truth is, the stain of death still clings to us. Just as Lazarus needed others to remove the wrappings from his body, we need the help of others in removing the stench of sin from ourselves. We cannot do this by ourselves. This is why God gave us his Church, to help us conquer sin.

> *Lord, set me totally free through your Church.*

Many who saw this, believed in Jesus while some went to the Pharisees. It is interesting that after raising Lazarus from the dead, the Pharisees and leaders plotted to kill Jesus.

They wanted to kill Life himself. By the death of one, everyone was saved. By dying, Jesus was able to give life. The seed had to be planted to bear fruit.

> *Lord, thank you for giving me life. Thank you for giving me hope. Thank you for giving yourself to me. Lord, you are the life I long for. You are the life I want. You are the life I need. Come and fill my heart. Come in to my life O Lord.*

Chapter 12

The Glory Begins

Six days before Passover, Mary anointed the feet of Jesus. Mary used "*a pound of ointment of pure nard, very precious*". Mary did not think of the cost. Just as the fragrance of the perfume filled the room, the death of Jesus would fill all creation. His death will redeem all creation and give it life.

Judas complained about this extravagance. He said, "*Why wasn't this ointment sold for three hundred denarii, and given to the poor?*" By saying this, Judas gave us an idea of how much the perfume cost. One denarii was equivalent to a day's wage during those times. Three hundred denarii is therefore, the cost of a person's wage for a year. Imagine a year's wage for one pound of perfume. Now THAT is expensive!

Jesus answered Judas and said the anointing was preparation for his burial. Anointing Jesus is more important than feeding the poor or any other work of charity. Believing in Jesus is more important than anything else.

One of the mistakes I had when I first came back to the Lord, was to think my works can save me. I thought being a Christian was to do good. However, as I got to know Jesus, I realized being a Christian is first and foremost, knowing Jesus. Doing good works is the fruit of knowing Jesus.

My good works will not save me. Only Jesus can and will save me. I need good works to perfect my faith. My good works are proof of what Jesus did for me. So giving to the poor is good and commendable. Other good works are good and commendable. But these do not compare to having a personal relationship with Jesus. Our relationship with Jesus comes first before anything else.

When one knows Jesus, one will know what to do. The priorities will be set right. The result is good deeds.

The chief priests wanted to kill Jesus. They also wanted to kill Lazarus. Many Jews believed in Jesus because of Lazarus.

The chief priests were righteous in terms of obeying the law. They did a lot of good works. And yet, they planned to kill Jesus AND Lazarus!

Their good works meant nothing because they would not accept what Jesus told them. They were blinded by their pride. In fact, their zeal for doing good led them to break the Law.

> *Teach me Lord to focus on you. Lead me Lord to do your will so I can truly live my life according to your Father's will. Let me arrange my priorities according to yours O Lord. Remind me that salvation comes from you alone - Jesus Christ - the Son of the Living God!*

JESUS: THE TRIUMPHANT KING

Five days before Passover, Jesus entered Jerusalem. His passion begins.

As he entered Jerusalem, he was given a triumphant entry. Everyone proclaimed him as king. In fulfillment of scripture, he entered Jerusalem while sitting on a young donkey. Unlike in previous instances where he hid himself when people wanted to make him king, this time, he allowed people to proclaim him as king. The people continued to testify that Jesus raised Lazarus from the dead. Because of this testimony, more joined the crowd.

THE WORLD GOES TO JESUS

The Pharisees were saying everyone was going to him. Jesus had not yet risen from the dead, but people were already going to him. Even the Greeks went to him. They approached Philip who took them to Andrew. In turn, Andrew took them to Jesus. The coming of the Gentiles to Jesus signified the time of glory, when ALL - even the non-Jews go to him.

Jesus then talked of a grain of wheat dying before it can bear fruit. One must die to have eternal life. This death is death to self, death to sin. Anyone who serves Jesus should follow him. Wherever Jesus is, his servant is there. God will honor those who serve Jesus.

> *Lord, let me die to myself. Let me die to my sinfulness. Let me die to what I want. Take my life and do to it as you wish. May my life honor you Lord. May I follow you and give glory to the Father through you.*

VICTORY AND GLORY

Jesus then said his time was here. He was troubled, but he looked forward to the completion of his time. By his death, the Father was glorified. Jesus was troubled, but he prayed for the Father's name to be glorified.

Similarly, when we are troubled, it is the time for God to be glorified.

The Father had glorified his name and will glorify it. When did he first glorify his Father's name? It was in the raising of Lazarus, in the healing of the blind man, in the healing of the lame man. God was glorified. Now, he will glorify it again, with the death and resurrection of Jesus. The voice was not for Jesus, but it was for those who heard it. Jesus said, *"Now is the judgment of this world. Now is the prince of this world cast out."*

Even before his death, Jesus had won the victory. Similarly, when we are in difficulties, we have won the victory. Victory in difficulties through Jesus!

St. Paul said we are more than conquerors in Christ. We are not "mere" conquerors, we are more than that! We are children of God, destined for glory!

> *Let me live this life of glory and victory O Lord. Through difficulties, I achieve victory and your glory is seen. Father, I want to live as your child. I want to get back the dignity you have planned for me even before the world began. Father, fulfill your plan in my life! Victory in Jesus is all I want. I want to glorify the Father. You are all I want!*

Jesus said *"And I, if I am lifted up from the earth, will draw all people to myself."* Jesus had to be lifted up from the earth. He had to be glorified. He had to be exalted over all so he could draw people to himself.

When preaching, one must remember to preach Jesus - not what one believes. This is how one can draw people to Jesus.

LIGHT AND DARKNESS

The Jewish leaders again started to ask - how can the Son of Man die, when he will remain forever? Jesus then spoke of light and darkness. While there is light, walk in the light. Those walking in darkness do not know where they are going. Believe in the light. Jesus then hid himself after saying this.

The Light hid himself so the leaders could not see. God *"has blinded their eyes and hardened their heart, lest they should see with their eyes and perceive with their heart, and would turn, and I would heal them."*

These words were spoken by Isaiah when he had a vision (Isaiah 6). Personally, I think the original words were spoken to teach the people of Israel the importance of seeing and understanding God. God was not responsible for their hard hearts. The people were. God was saying if they see and perceive with their hearts, then he would heal them. But the people would not see. They chose not to see and therefore, they chose to reject the healing of God.

> *Lord, I want to choose you. Heal me, let me see.*

SEEING JESUS

Many of the leaders believed in Jesus, but they did not speak out because they were afraid of men. Indeed, our confession will depend on who we want to please.

Hardness of heart is caused by unbelief. Seeing Jesus is a gift from God. Only God can reveal Jesus and we have to respond. If I cannot see Jesus and am sincere, I have to ask God and be open to him. I cannot see if I do not admit blindness. Only God can heal and if I do not ask God to heal me, I cannot be healed.

To believe in Jesus is to believe in the Father. To see Jesus is to see the Father. Jesus is the Light. Believing in Jesus brings light.

> *Lord, I want to see you. Reveal yourself to me. May I surrender my life to you. Teach me Lord, to come to the Light – to come to you. Let me see so you can heal me. If my heart is hard, break it Lord. Change my heart of stone into a heart of flesh. You are my Lord. You are my God. I believe in you.*

Chapter 13

Prepared for Glory

Jesus loved his own who were in the world. He loved them to the end. There is no end to God's love. At this point, Jesus knew the Father had given everything into his hands. He now has control of everything. He knew he came from the Father and was going back to him.

Jesus rose from the table, removed his outer garment, took a towel and wrapped it around his waist. He poured water into a basin. He stooped down to wash their feet. He took the towel and wiped the feet of his disciples.

Jesus came down from heaven. He removed his glory and wrapped on human flesh. He stooped down to pour water and then washed their feet. This reminds me of the waters of creation. God "stooped" from heaven to form man from the dust of the ground. By his towel, Jesus cleaned the disciples. By his blood, by his humanity, he washed us clean.

A Servant God

God is a serving God. It is in his nature to serve. He serves because he loves. Peter would not allow Jesus to wash his feet. But Jesus said, "*If I don't wash you, you have no part with me*." On hearing this, Peter wanted Jesus to wash his whole body.

The washing of the feet was done by the lowest of slaves. By doing this, Jesus must have shocked his disciples. He was taking on the place of the lowest of slaves.

Jesus came to wash our feet. He took on the form of a slave to save us.

> *Lord, what a wonderful God you are. The Almighty*
> *God, who created the universe, came to die for me.*
> *He continues to give himself to me through the*
> *Eucharist. He continues to serve me. Lord, wash me*
> *and cleanse me.*

Jesus said, *"Someone who has bathed only needs to have his feet washed, but is completely clean. You are clean, but not all of you."* Jesus washed the disciples' feet, including Judas' feet. According to Jesus, the condition for being clean is to have bathed first. Then he said not all are clean.

Although Jesus washed Judas' feet, Judas was not clean because he had not washed himself. He had to repent first before he could be forgiven.

Salvation is a gift. God has given that gift. We are invited to respond to that gift. Everyone has to make a decision on whether they want to accept the cleansing of Jesus. If there is no decision to accept that gift, then we remain unclean.

After Jesus washed their feet, he took off the towel and put on his outer garment. This is symbolic of him, giving up his life and taking on the glory of the Father.

Jesus gave an example of service - humility - taking off his glory to become man. One has to follow Jesus - not only by serving others, but by giving up his glory and taking on flesh - to be obedient to the Father and to seek the glory of the Father.

> *Lord, may I truly seek to do your glory. Jesus, help*
> *me to see you and obey the Father's will.*

The servant cannot be greater than his master. *"If you know these things, blessed are you if you do them."* One must know where one stands before Jesus. Judas did not know where he stood. He did not know his place. Jesus is the Lord, we are his creation. Judas did not want to submit to Jesus. He did not believe in Jesus. That was why he betrayed Jesus.

Jesus foretold this to prove that HE IS. Who is Jesus? He is one with the Father. The Father and Jesus are one. When Judas betrayed Jesus, he also betrayed the Father. When Jesus served the disciples, the Father also served the disciples. What Jesus said are the words of the Father.

THE PASSION AND VICTORY

Satan entered Judas when he took the bread from Jesus. When Jesus spoke to Judas, he was speaking to Satan. He told Satan to do quickly what he had to do. From this perspective, it seemed like Jesus was telling Satan "do your worst now. Do it quickly so victory can be achieved quickly." Jesus is ALWAYS victorious!

When Satan started the events that would lead to the death of Jesus, Jesus already declared victory. The Son of God *HAS* been glorified. Even when the death had not happened, Jesus had already won!

When Satan entered Judas, evening came. It was now the darkest hour. But Jesus said at this time, *"Now the Son of Man has been glorified, and God has been glorified in him. If God has been glorified in him, God will also glorify him in himself, and he will glorify him immediately."* In the darkest hour, Jesus was glorified and so was the Father with him and God will glorify Jesus immediately.

This is the victory we have with Jesus. In the midst of difficulties, we are already victorious. God will glorify his children immediately. The key word here is *"immediately"*.

God is glorified when we love one another. Our goal is to glorify God - by the love we show each other.

> *Father, through my life's difficulties, through my sinfulness, through the darkness in my life, let me see the victory you have prepared for me. I am more than a conqueror. I am your child - whom you love so much. You have redeemed me Lord. Come and restore to me the glory you have planned for me.*

Trust in God

"*Don't let your heart be troubled. Believe in God. Believe also in me.*" There are three commands as we begin Chapter 14. First, Jesus commands us not to be troubled. Then he commands us to believe in the Father and lastly, to believe in him.

The word translated as "*troubled*" means to agitate, to stir up. With this, Jesus commands us not to be so agitated. Do not be so worried. When things go wrong, when things do not meet our expectations, when we are disappointed and fearful, settle down! Trust in God. Trust in Jesus.

In the midst of difficulties, we continue to trust in God. Jesus goes to prepare a place for us. If this were not so, he would have told us. Jesus does not lie. When he goes, he will return at the right time. He does this so we may be where he is.

Jesus wants us to live with him in his Father's house. If this was not God's plan, he would have told us. God's plan is for us to live with him. This is why Jesus said he will take us to the Father's house.

Jesus said, "*I will come again, and will receive you to myself; that where I am, you may be there also.*" Therefore, the way to him is to wait for him. When difficulties come, we struggle against it; believing the words of Jesus. He will come and help us. He will come and receive us so we may be with him.

Thomas said he did not know where Jesus was going so he did not know the way. Jesus' answer implied where he was going was not important.

What matters is Jesus himself. He is the Way. He went to the Father and this is also our destiny. We can only go to the Father through Jesus.

> *Lord, may I respond to your grace to trust in you. May I be bold enough to trust in you. May I be bold enough to wait for you and follow you wherever you lead. I know if I trust you, I shall know the Father.*

ASK IN THE NAME OF JESUS

Philip wanted to see the Father. In answer, Jesus revealed his unity with the Father. To see Jesus is to see the Father. To hear Jesus is to hear the Father. To believe in Jesus is to believe in the Father. If one finds it hard to believe in Jesus, one can look at what he did. Believe in his works. His works always point to Jesus.

The one who believes Jesus will do greater things than Jesus. This is possible because Jesus was going to the Father. Jesus promised, *"Whatever you will ask in my name, that will I do, that the Father may be glorified in the Son."*

Whatever we ask in his name, he will do. This is for one purpose: to glorify the Father. This is the purpose of our lives - to give glory to the Father.

To ask in Jesus' name is to ask what he will ask. It is to be one with the will of the Father. Because Jesus is one with the Father, what he asks is always in the will of the Father.

> *Jesus, thank you for teaching me to ask from the Father and for the assurance the Father will give me what I ask in your name. Give me the confidence to seek the Father's will - to seek his glory.*

The Holy Spirit

Loving Jesus is loving the Father. Jesus reveals himself to those who love him. The proof of our love for Jesus is obedience to him. He tells us what he wants and if we love him, we will obey him. When we love Jesus, he will pray to the Father to send the Holy Spirit. The Holy Spirit will be with us forever.

The Holy Spirit is the Spirit of Truth. The world does not see him or know him. But he lives in us and will be with us. The Spirit will never leave us. Where the Holy Spirit is, Jesus and the Father are there. Jesus will leave but we shall see him because we believe. We live according to the power of the Holy Spirit.

Anyone who follows Jesus loves him. The Father and Jesus will dwell in him. What does this mean? The Father and Jesus will make us their home. They will live and rule in us. We will have fellowship with them. The Spirit will teach ALL things and will remind us of ALL things. The Spirit is the one who teaches us.

> *Holy Spirit of Truth, come with your power. Come and lead me to Jesus, the Truth. Live in me and be with me. Let me see Jesus. Teach me all things and remind me of all things. Come Lord, let me see Jesus.*

The Peace of Jesus

Jesus gives his peace. In the midst of trouble, we shall have peace because we know Jesus is in control. This is a command: *"Don't let your heart be troubled, neither let it be fearful."*

The phrase: *"Don't let your hearts be troubled"* is repeated twice in this chapter. God's word is important - this is why scripture is vital to one's life. If something is mentioned twice in scripture, then it requires much attention.

Since this phrase occurs twice in this chapter, it needs some attention. As mentioned earlier, the word translated as *"troubled"* means to stir up sediments so the water becomes unclear.

Jesus commands us to keep our minds clear. We should not cloud our hearts that we become confused. Instead, our hearts should remain steadfast - faithful to God.

Jesus also commands us not to be afraid. Often, when our hearts are troubled, we start to worry. When Jesus was about to die, he commanded his disciples to remain steadfast and not to be afraid. They needed to trust him, to trust his word so they could have peace.

We too should trust in the words of Jesus. When difficulties and uncertainties come, our only hope is in the words of Jesus - he will never abandon us. We find confidence by trusting in God's word.

> *Lord, you command me not to be troubled. You command me not to be afraid. Indeed Lord, the only way to have peace is to hold to your word. Teach me to hold on to your word so I may have peace.*

"If you loved me, you would have rejoiced, because I said 'I am going to my Father;'". If we love Jesus, we will want the best for him. His going to the Father was the best for him. Although the disciples wanted him to be with them physically, he had to go to the Father.

In life, we will have troubles. Jesus will seem to abandon us. It would seem like he has left us. But we believe, we know, he will come again. The Spirit will always remind us of the promises of Jesus. He will teach us everything we need to know when trouble comes. Troubles have to come so we can see the power of the Holy Spirit. When Jesus leaves - he sends the Holy Spirit.

His words are also signs to prove he is in control. Evil will come but it does not have any hold on Jesus.

Jesus is more powerful than the Evil One and the Evil One had no hold over him. Because of this, Jesus was ready to face him. He told his disciples to stand and he led them on.

When confronted by evil, we will not be afraid. We stand with Jesus, ready so he can lead us to confront the Evil One.

> *Lord, I want the peace only you can give. In the midst of trouble and difficulties, send your Holy Spirit to quicken my spirit. Holy Spirit, remind me of the promises of Jesus. May I find comfort in his words. Holy Spirit, be my strength. Lead me to Jesus - ALWAYS!*

Chapter 15

Stand Firm in Jesus

Jesus says he is the true vine and the Father is the gardener. Jesus is THE vine. He is not a vine. There is only one TRUE vine - and that vine is Jesus.

This means there are many false vines. These are vines that claim to also help us bear fruit. One may still bear fruit through these, but only Jesus makes us bear fruit - in abundance - with fruit that will last.

> *How many times Lord, have I searched for you in things. How many times Lord, have I tried to do things without you. Let me cling to you Jesus. I want to bear fruit in you and for you. I want to bear fruit that will last. I want to bear these in abundance.*

The Father is the one who determines which branch stays with Jesus and which one is cut off. The reason for staying with Jesus is to bear fruit. For those that bear fruit, the Father prunes so they may bear more fruit. We are cleansed by the words of Jesus. Jesus tells us to remain in him.

The dictionary says to *remain* is "to stand, to tarry". To remain in Jesus is to stand in Jesus, to be firm in Jesus. To stand; not walk, not sit, but stand.

We only bear fruit if we stand in Jesus, wait for him to nourish us, and cling to him. If we remain in Jesus, we bear fruit. We cannot bear fruit by ourselves.

To stand in Jesus is to be firm in him; to hope in him. When we stand firm in Jesus, we grow. We receive nourishment. If we do not stand in Jesus, we will surely die. We cannot bear fruit without Jesus. Isaiah says, *"If you will not believe, surely you shall not be established"* (Isaiah 7:9).

If we stand firm in Jesus and his word is firmly in us, then we can ask what we wish and it will be given. The word of Jesus should be firmly set in us. It is our nourishment. It will let us bear fruit. It gives us confidence that God is with us. This happens for the glory of God.

> *Lord, teach me to stand in you. Teach me to rely on you. May I bear fruit in abundance for the glory of the Father.*

THE LOVE OF JESUS

Jesus loves us as the Father loves him. This is a profound statement. The Father loves Jesus infinitely and perfectly. Jesus loves us infinitely and perfectly. Jesus commands us to stand in him. To stand in Jesus is to keep his commandments - to remain firmly committed to him - to do what he commands.

His command was to love one another as he loves us. He was willing to die for others. His call was for us to do the same. This is the only way for us to remain in him.

How much do we love others - even our enemies? Am I willing to die for them? This is one of the more difficult commands from Jesus. We can do this only by the grace of God.

When we remain in Jesus, we will not only have joy. Our joy will be complete. Joy is a gift from Jesus. This is the will of God - that we may be full of joy. This joy continues in the midst of hatred from the world. Even if people are against us, we will still have joy because we stand in Jesus. Joy is not an emotion. It is knowing we are doing God's will and he is in control.

> *Lord, I want joy in my life - the joy only you can give.*
> *This joy gives me confidence in whatever situation.*
> *In the midst of persecution, in the midst of*
> *difficulties, in the midst of trouble, give me this joy*
> *and may I have it in abundance!*

FRIENDS OF JESUS

Jesus tells us to love one another. To love one another is difficult enough. But to love one another as he loves us is humanly impossible. It is possible only by grace. Jesus showed his love to his disciples by dying for them. He gave his life for his friends. The friends of Jesus are those who do what he says - those who obey him.

The proof that we are friends of Jesus is when he tells us everything he heard from the Father. God does not speak in chaos. He speaks clearly and he tells us everything!

Jesus chooses us and he sends us to bear fruit that will last. When this becomes our goal, we can ask the Father for anything and it shall be given.

> *Lord, may I always respond to your grace so I may*
> *bear fruit, fruit that will last and fruit in abundance,*
> *for the glory of the Father.*

JOY

The joy from Jesus comes from the hope that God will intervene. If Jesus was hated by the sinful world, those who follow him will also be hated. This is expected. We are not of the world. The important thing is Jesus loves us. Even when the world hates us, Jesus loves us. This is enough.

People hated Jesus for no reason at all. We are to expect this also. People will hate us for no reason at all.

The important thing is Jesus will send the Counselor - the Holy Spirit of Truth. The Spirit will testify about Jesus and we too will testify about Jesus.

> *Lord, I am confident you are in control of my life. Give me joy O Lord - which is confidence that you are here with me. Holy Spirit, remind me of the truth. May I cling to Jesus as my Savior in the midst of all my difficulties. Let me not run to others thinking they can save me. But remind me of the truth that only Jesus can save me and my salvation rests in trusting him alone.*

Chapter 16

Victory of Jesus

Jesus now warned his disciples of what will happen. They would be thrown out of their synagogues. People would think they are doing good when they kill his friends.

Jesus said all these things so we may know he is in control. He knows what will happen and he knows how to deal with these.

He did not say this to his disciples before because he was with them. It was not time for them to be exposed to these. Jesus was still there to protect them. But now, Jesus was leaving them. It would be their time at the front line.

THE HOLY SPIRIT COMES

Jesus had to go for the Spirit to come.

In life, in the midst of trouble, we will suffer. These sufferings allow the Spirit to come and redeem us - to give us power. When we are weak, we are strong. In our darkest, God's light shines the brightest even if we do not see it. We do not see, not because of the darkness, but because we are blinded by the light.

The Spirit convicts the world about sin, of righteousness and judgment. Sin is not believing in Jesus. Righteousness is seen because Jesus rose from the dead and is going to the Father. The resurrection of Jesus showed who was right - Jesus or the leaders. Judgment - because the prince of this world stands condemned. The condemnation of Satan is proof of judgment. The Holy Spirit will reveal all these things to us.

THE SPIRIT REVEALS

Jesus had many things to say, but what he had to say was
too much for his disciples to bear. God does not reveal
everything to us in one instant. He reveals these slowly
and at the appropriate time. The Spirit leads us to all truth.
He speaks for Jesus. He tells us what is to come. He
glorifies Jesus. He takes from Jesus what he tells us.

When the Spirit takes from Jesus, he is taking from the
Father because all the Father has belongs to Jesus.

Jesus said, *"A little while, and you won't see me, and
again a little while, and you will see me."* When Jesus
shows himself, then the sorrow will turn to joy.

In life, there will be difficulties. God will seem absent. The
best time for prayer is in the midst of our difficulties
because that is when the Father is closest to us. This is the
moment when we are one with the Father's will.

There is a guarantee this will turn to joy, because we will
see him. When that time comes, our joy will be full - such
that no one can take it away from us.

*Lord Jesus, when you seem absent, when things are
dark, may your Spirit remind me of your presence.
May the darkness teach me to trust in you, to hold on
to you. May it strengthen my faith as I trust in you.
May I look to the hope you will intervene. May my
joy be based on this hope O Lord.*

ASK ANYTHING IN JESUS' NAME

When our joy is full, then only Jesus matters. There will
be no more questions because we have seen the love of our
lives. We will know and be one with the Father's will.

Then we will ask anything from the Father. At that time, the only one that matters is Jesus. We will ask the Father for Jesus and he will give him to us.

Jesus told the disciples to ask anything in his name. In the midst of their sorrow, Jesus told them to ask in his name. In the midst of our difficulties, Jesus tells us to ask in his name. Look within and see what Jesus wants you to ask at this point in your life. Ask Jesus and it shall be given.

> *Lord, may I know you intimately so I can ask you anything. May I be bold to stand before you and ask anything in your name. More importantly, may I always be in you so I can know what to ask. Reveal the Father to me Lord.*

During our sorrows, we will not understand what Jesus is saying or doing. But when we see him, when our joy is full, Jesus will reveal the Father. This is possible because the Father loves those who believe in Jesus. Understanding Jesus is not important. What is important is seeing Jesus through faith; knowing he is there.

Jesus knew the disciples believed he came from the Father. God knows our inmost thoughts. He knows us deeply, more than we know ourselves.

With this, Jesus questioned their belief. He said they would leave him by himself. But in the midst of this abandonment, Jesus knew the Father was with him. That was enough for him.

Jesus said all these so his disciples might have peace. In the midst of our difficulties, Jesus is in control. When God seems to be losing, that is when we need to hold on. There will be troubles, but Jesus HAS already won the war.

Notice what Jesus said. He had not yet been crucified, he had not yet risen from the dead, but he said, *"Cheer up, I have overcome the world!"* Even when we face difficulties, Jesus has won. The battle has not started, we already know the victor. He is Jesus Christ, the Son of the Living God!

Since we are in Jesus, we also have that victory. This is why St. Paul said we are more than conquerors in Christ!

Father, indeed, you are all that matters. You are enough. Even when others abandon me, remind me that you are there. Though my father and mother abandon me, you O Lord are always there. This is enough for me. You are the Almighty God who is always victorious! Lead me to your victory my God!

Chapter 17

Infinite Glory

This chapter begins the priestly prayer of Jesus. Jesus asked the Father to glorify him! Since this was the prayer of Jesus, this was the will of the Father. Does the Father want to glorify us too?

Yes of course! We are his adopted children. As such, we are co-heirs with Jesus. As co-heirs, we are entitled to all Jesus has, as long as we share in his sufferings. This is also what the Father wants for us. He wants to bless us, he wants to glorify us and he wants to give us eternal life.

The Father gave Jesus authority over all flesh. Because of his authority, Jesus is able to give eternal life. Jesus defines eternal life as *"knowing the One True God and Jesus Christ"*. Eternal life is having an intimate relationship with Jesus and his Father.

Jesus spoke in the past tense. *"I glorified you and have accomplished the work you have given me to do."* When Jesus had done what the Father wanted, he could ask for anything. And he asked BIG TIME *"Now, Father, glorify me with your own self with the glory which I had with you before the world existed."* Jesus asked his Father to glorify him infinitely!

With this prayer, Jesus showed us how to ask in prayer: we need to ask BIG! Do not be content with asking for small things. Ask the Father for great and wonderful things! Since, as St. Paul said, *"Things which an eye didn't see, and an ear didn't hear, which didn't enter into the heart of man, these God has prepared for those who love him"* (2

Corinthians 2:9). God has planned something for us since the beginning. We can ask the Father to fulfill what he has planned for us. This is something that is beyond our dreams and imagination!

> *Father, let me be the person you want me to be. Let me receive everything you have planned for me since the beginning of time. Let me be open to you - so I can fulfill what you have created me to be. Let me know you, the One True God and Jesus, so I may have eternal life.*

Jesus did not want anyone to glorify him. He wanted the Father to glorify him. This is also what we should ask. To ask for anything less is to cheat ourselves. We should not settle for anything less!

BELONG TO JESUS

Jesus reveals the Father to those whom the Father has given him. Those the Father gave to Jesus belong to Jesus.

Those who belong to Jesus obey the Father. They know the Father is above all things and he has given all these to Jesus. They also receive the word given by the Father. They nurture it and make it part of their lives. Because of this, they know, without doubt, Jesus came from the Father and he is one with the Father. They believe the Father sent Jesus to redeem the world.

> *Jesus, take me as your own. Guide me to you always. You are enough for me. You are all I need and want. I know and believe you came from the Father.*

Why did Jesus pray only for those who belong to him and not for everyone? Those who belong to the Father need protection from the world. Those who do not belong to the Father do not need protection. The enemy aims to take back those who used to belong to him and now belong to the Father.

Life is a battle between good and evil, between God and Satan. For those who choose God, God is faithful. However, Satan will do everything to deceive them. It is not a question of who one chooses, but of discerning whose voice one is following. Those in Jesus will never consciously choose to follow the voice of the enemy. They will choose to follow God. However, there is nothing to prevent the enemy from trying to deceive them. This is why Jesus prayed for them.

UNITY

Those who belong to the Father glorify him. Jesus prayed for their unity. Not any kind of unity, but to be united perfectly as he is united with the Father. Unity here means to be of the same mind. Jesus submitted to the Father. For the Church to be united, every member has to have the same mind as Jesus - to do the Father's will.

When he was with the disciples, Jesus was the uniting force. He protected them from harm. This is the source of joy for those who belong to Jesus. This is no ordinary joy, it is a full, complete and perfect joy. Knowing Jesus protects us. Jesus has given us his word. This word protects us.

> *Lord, protect me from the enemy. Protect me by your word. Instill in me the love for your word.*

We are not meant to withdraw from the world. We are meant to be in the world. This is why Jesus asked the Father to protect us from the Evil One. We are sanctified, that means separated, from the world by the truth. Those in Jesus are in the world. They are not called to be **OF** the world. They are to act apart from the world; to be counter-cultural so they can truly give glory to the Father.

This life is possible only through the word of God. God's word is the truth. Jesus sends us as the Father sent him - into the world. Jesus has shown how he separated himself from the world. We learn from Jesus. We are separated from the world by the truth as revealed by God.

Jesus now shifted his focus to those who will believe because of the apostles. The oneness of the believers in Jesus will make the world believe the Father sent him. Jesus gave the same glory he received from the Father to those who belong to him - for the purpose of these being united in one will.

THE SAME GLORY AS JESUS

This is an amazing thought. We receive the same glory Jesus received from the Father. This is an infinite glory! The intention of this is so the world may know the Father sent Jesus and he loves those who belong to him - just as he loves Jesus!

The people whom Jesus prayed for were those who belong to him and not those who believe in him. There seems to be a difference between believing in Jesus and belonging to Jesus. Believing in Jesus is the start. It allows access to eternal life.

To belong to Jesus is to share his glory! Those who belong to Jesus have fellowship with him. The Samaritan town in Chapter 4 believed in Jesus - so they came to him. But the disciples belonged to Jesus because they had a deeper relationship with him.

Believing is the first step. Belonging is the completion or perfection of that first step. When one belongs to Jesus, one is "owned" by Jesus and therefore, is under his protection.

Jesus wants us to be with him, so we can see his glory. The Father sent Jesus. He loved Jesus since the beginning. Jesus knows the Father infinitely. Those who belong to Jesus know the Father sent Jesus. Jesus revealed his Father to those who belong to him so we may have the love of the Father through Jesus.

> *Lord, may I respond to your call. I want to believe in you. I want to belong to you Lord. Take me as I am and give me the glory you have. Use me Lord, for the glory of the Father.*

Chapter 18

Jesus is in Control

After saying his prayer, Jesus and his disciples went to a garden. Judas also came with soldiers and officers and they brought lanterns, torches and weapons. This is quite interesting because Adam and Eve were in a garden and the serpent also came to the garden. Jesus is the true Light and John mentioned about the soldiers and officers coming with some light.

Another translation (*Young's Literal Translation*) says Judas "*delivered*" Jesus to the soldiers and officers. It was as if Judas had possession of Jesus and he brought Jesus to them.

When Jesus saw the mob coming, he confronted them. He asked them who they were looking for. When they answered they were looking for "*Jesus of Nazareth*", Jesus replied, "*I am he.*" His response, although translated as "*I am he*" was actually, "*I AM*". Jesus told them who he was, he was God! Because of this, the mob stepped backward and fell to the ground.

In the Garden of Eden, Adam was with Eve and he let her confront the serpent on her own. In this garden, Jesus, the new Adam, was there to confront evil. When he faced evil, he did not hide in fear. Instead, he faced it squarely and boldly - showing he was in control.

> *Lord, when I am confronted by evil, be with me to defend me for I am weak. Let me not trust in my own power. Instead, let me confront them with you.*

He asked them a second time, and they replied the same. Jesus told them they were looking for him and he told them to let the others go. In the garden, Adam left Eve by herself with the serpent. Even when Eve ate the fruit, he did not confront her. He even gave in to her. But here, Jesus confronted evil and sought to protect those that were his so none would be lost.

The Battle Begins

Peter saw this as the "sign" to start to fight. Peter drew his sword and struck the high priest's servant, Malchus. Malchus is a Hebrew name taken from the word *Melek* which means *King*.

This *king* turned out to be a servant, a pretender. Peter struck their "*king*". The Prince of the Apostles was waging a war against the 'pretender-king'. But Jesus told him to put the sword down because this was his battle. When confronted by evil, the battle we fight is not our own. We are soldiers, waiting for Jesus to fight. Jesus fights for us. He is always there to confront evil. We fight evil based on how Jesus would want to. We listen to our commander.

With this, the soldiers, officers and commanding officer seized Jesus and bound him. The commanding officer was not just a commanding officer. Literally, he was the commander of a thousand soldiers.

The root word for commanding officer meant a thousand, thousands. With this, John drew a picture of Jesus against a thousand soldiers - and still, Jesus was in control. God faced the thousand, thousands of the army of evil.

In this, God seemed to lose. They had him. They bound him and had control of him.

In our difficulties, when we are overwhelmed, when we feel evil has triumphed, we look back to this scene.

Thousands and thousands bound the Son of God, yet he was in control!

God is always in control of our situation! In the end, we shall overcome, we shall be victorious.

> *Yes Lord. In the midst of difficulties and sufferings, let me remember you are in control. Jesus, you alone faced a thousand, thousands, yet you were still in control. It may look like they have won. But in the end, you shall prove victorious.*

THE TRIAL OF JESUS

They brought Jesus to Annas. His name comes from the Hebrew *Hananaiah*, which means *God has favored*. This is interesting because Satan used to be Lucifer, God's favorite angel before he rebelled against God. Annas was the father-in-law of Caiaphas. The name Caiaphas means a dell - *a secluded hollow or small valley usually covered with trees or turf* (Merriam-Webster dictionary).

A disciple known to the high priest entered the court with Jesus. Peter was outside and the disciple went out and told the woman at the door to let Peter in. The woman asked Peter if he was a disciple of Jesus. Peter denied it.

At this point, Jesus, the disciple and Peter were in the court. The soldiers were in the court warming themselves at the fire. Peter stood with them, warming himself.

Now, the trial begins.

GOD REVEALS HIMSELF

Jesus was presented to Annas, *God's favored.* God was before Satan himself. Annas asked Jesus about his disciples and his teachings. Jesus said he taught openly, he did not say anything in secret.

When God speaks, he says nothing in secret. Jesus speaks the truth openly. God reveals himself truthfully and openly. He does not speak in riddles. He reveals and speaks plainly. There is no reason not to believe him.

> *Lord, may I see you as you reveal yourself to me.*
> *May my perceptions and preconceived ideas not*
> *cloud your revelation. May I accept you as you are.*

The officer did not like what he heard so he slapped Jesus. Jesus responded that he spoke no evil so therefore, did not deserve it. The discussion ended there and Annas sent Jesus to Caiaphas. Jesus was still bound.

Peter was standing with the soldiers and they asked him if he was one of Jesus' disciples. Peter again denied it. One of the relatives of Malchus asked Peter if he saw him in the garden with Jesus. Peter again denied it and the rooster crowed. After Peter denied Jesus, evening passed. Morning begins. The darkness will slowly be defeated.

Peter's denial of Jesus was the lowest point of his faith. Yet, it was after his denial that morning began. In our life, when we are at our lowest, that is when God begins to lift up the darkness.

THE MORNING BEGINS

Caiaphas was with Pilate in the Praetorium very early in the morning. It is ironic the chief priests and leaders did not want to defile themselves but here they were, before God himself!

They were abusing him and plotting to kill him. They wanted to be ritually clean to eat the Passover Lamb, but they had no problem killing an innocent man. They had to kill the true Passover Lamb first before they could eat it. They had to kill God's Lamb before they could be saved from death.

Pilate came out and asked them about their charges against Jesus. They did not say anything except Jesus was an evil doer. Pilate did not want to deal with the issue but they persisted and said they wanted to crucify Jesus. They brought Jesus to Pilate so he could sentence Jesus to death, because only the Romans had authority to crucify anyone. The leaders wanted what was lawful, but not what was right.

> *Lord, let me do what is right. Let me see you and honor you. Guide me Jesus in all I do. Let me not be bound by human traditions. Instead, let me see you as you are. Remove whatever prevents me from seeing you Lord.*

THE KING OF THE JEWS

Pilate entered the Praetorium and asked Jesus, *"Are you the King of the Jews?"* Pilate probably heard of rumors about this man from Nazareth who entered Jerusalem a few days ago as a king. If he was the king of the Jews, then he should be crucified. Jesus' reply was interesting.

He did not answer Pilate's question, but he asked a question, *"Do you say this by yourself or did others tell you?"* In this trial, Pilate was supposed to be the judge. But Jesus was the one asking the questions. He was not asking the questions to clarify something. He was asking the question for Pilate to answer.

We too have to answer these questions: Is Jesus my King? Do I say this because others say so or is it based on my conviction? Who is Jesus? Do I know him because someone told me or do I know him because I really know him?

> *Lord, who are you to me? Let me answer that question truthfully. Remove whatever blinds me from seeing who you are. Lord, come; because I want to know who you are. I want to accept you as my King.*

Pilate replied with two questions. *"I'm not a Jew, am I? Your own nation and the chief priests delivered you to me. What have you done?"*

Jesus said his kingdom was not from this world. If it was, his followers would fight and he would not have been delivered to the Jews. He did not say he was delivered to Pilate, but he was delivered to the Jews. Pilate then asked Jesus again, *"Are you a king then?"*

What is Truth?

Jesus told Pilate his mission: he did not come to rule the world. He came to testify to the truth. He added, anyone who is of the truth listens to his voice. Pilate was probably frustrated and said, *"What is truth?"* This is another question everyone has to answer. What truth was Jesus talking about?

Many people today claim to know the truth. There are issues on morality and ethics that conflict with God's original plan. We have our own truth. God has his own truth. In the end, whose truth really matters?

In John 7:18, Jesus said *"He who speaks from himself seeks his own glory, but he who seeks the glory of him who sent him is true, and no unrighteousness is in him."*

He also spoke of the Spirit, *"for he will not speak from himself; but whatever he hears, he will speak. He will declare to you things that are coming"* (John 16:13).

The truth is what comes from God. Jesus speaks whatever comes from the Father. He works for the glory of the one who sent him. Jesus is the Truth. When Pilate asked,

"What is truth?", he was before Truth himself and he did not realize it.

> *How often have I come before you Lord, seeking your will, yet, right before me is your will? I would not accept it because it was not convenient and it was difficult. Your truth was not what I wanted to hear. It did not fit my wants. Lord, for those times, forgive me. Let me work for your glory. Let me accept your truth, no matter how difficult it is for me.*

Pilate went out and told the leaders he found no basis for crucifying Jesus and would like to release him. Pilate gave them the choice on whether they wanted to release their Messiah or not.

They choose Barabbas (which meant, *father's son*). They wanted a pretender and not the Truth. They wanted a robber instead of God.

This brings us back to Chapter 10. Jesus said, the thief comes to steal, kill and destroy. They were given a choice, the true Son of the Father or the false one. The one who came to give them life or the one who came to steal, kill and destroy. This was a choice between God and Satan. And they choose Satan.

Who should we choose? Who do we choose?

> *Very often, I am confronted with this choice. Do I want my true King or do I want a lie? Who is more important, Jesus or something else? Very often, I choose other things. Lord, have mercy on me. Let me choose you always.*

Chapter 19

King of the Jews

Pilate took Jesus and had him flogged. The soldiers dressed him up as a king. They gave him a crown of thorns and a purple garment. They kept saying, *"Hail, King of the Jews!"*, but they beat him. The right words were spoken, but the actions did not fit. They said these words to mock Jesus.

> *Jesus, I have often called you my Lord and King, yet, my actions do not speak so. My actions insult you and do not give glory to you. Lord, have mercy. I should know better. Yet, I don't. Help me. Save me!*

After the beating, Pilate brought Jesus out in full regalia: with a crown of thorns and a purple garment. Pilate wanted to show the crowd he had punished Jesus to appease them so he could release him. When Pilate said, *"Behold, the man!"* he was showing the crowd the punishment done to Jesus.

THE EFFECTS OF SIN

Here, we see how one looks when one lives in sin. St. Paul said *"For him who knew no sin he made to be sin on our behalf; so that in him we might become the righteousness of God"* (2 Corinthians 5:21).

What happened to Jesus physically is what happens spiritually to those who sin. One is beaten and insulted. The dignity is lost. God created man to be ruler of creation. But due to sin, man is beaten, bruised and near death. This is the sinful man.

When confronted by sin, the people rejected it. They did not want to see their sin. They did not want to see how disfigured they were from the image of God. They did not want to see how much they had lost. Because of this, they wanted to kill that Truth.

The people wanted to believe there was nothing wrong with them. Nobody wanted to see themselves disfigured. Jesus stood before them. He was showing them the horrible truth of what sin does to people.

They asked to crucify Jesus. They wanted to get rid of the image of sin. They wanted to retain their illusion of perfection.

How true this is of our lives. We sin and yet would not want to face sin. We see the consequence, yet would rather deny the truth than face it.

> *This is how I look when I live in sin. This is what sin does to me. It robs me of my dignity. It beats me to near death. It insults me. Yet, I would not want to accept this. I would prefer not to confront this and stay in my illusion of my righteousness. I am perfect by my own standard. Lord God, save me from myself.*

THE SON OF GOD

Pilate wanted to release Jesus, but the crowd kept insisting on death. The leaders said Jesus called himself the Son of God. Again, the right words, but they would not believe.

Here is another case of one believing in Jesus as God. Pilate believed Jesus was the Son of God. The gospel said *"When therefore Pilate heard this saying, he was more afraid."* He believed but this was not the believing Jesus was talking about.

Pilate's belief was not based on a loving relationship with Jesus. It was a relationship of fear and arrogance. He felt he was above Jesus, but the truth is Jesus was way beyond Pilate.

Part of believing in Jesus is not only in knowing he is the Son of God. It is in knowing where one stands before him.

> *Jesus, let me know where I stand before you. You are God, I am your creature. Always remind me of this.*

Pilate asked Jesus who he was, but as Jesus remained silent, he got frustrated and told him he had the power to release him or crucify him. Jesus said the power Pilate had was given by God.

Pilate boasted of what he had - power over life and death. He never realized the person who had the real power over life and death was before him! The trial was reversed. Now, Jesus was standing as the judge. Pilate was on trial. Jesus knew where he came from and Pilate did not. Pilate was torn between Jesus and the people. Jesus knew what he wanted to do - the Father's will. In all these, Jesus did not plead for his life. He left his life in the hands of the people, knowing this was the Father's will.

With regards to those who handed him over, he left it to the Father.

> *Lord, how often, I judge your works. I criticize you and even get frustrated when things do not go my way. I stand in judgment over you, not knowing you are the Eternal Judge. Let me desire to only do the Father's will. Jesus, teach me to forgive those who had done me wrong. Let the Father's justice deal with them.*

BEHOLD, YOUR KING

Pilate wanted to free Jesus but the chief priests said anyone who wanted to be king spoke against Caesar. Pilate then took the judgment seat. He said to the people,

"Behold, your King." John mentions it was the sixth hour, 12 noon. At the brightest time of day, Pilate made a revelation. But the people rejected Jesus. They wanted to crucify him. Pilate asked, *"Shall I crucify your King?"* They replied they had no king but Caesar.

Pilate called Jesus as the King of the Jews. Yet, he did so in an insulting manner. The soldiers also called him that to mock him. Pilate showed them a king who was beaten and near death, clothed with a purple garment and crowned with thorns. Pilate, even if he did not know it, was saying the right thing.

The chief priests and leaders, because of their hard hearts did not want Jesus as king. They rejected God as their king. Instead, they chose Caesar, a worldly king whom their enemies worshiped as a god.

In a reversal of roles, the pagans who did not know God professed Jesus as the King of the Jews. The Jewish leaders who knew God rejected him. They could not see him. They preferred a human king rather than their One True King.

This is the ultimate idolatry. God was before them, yet they choose an idol. When we are confronted with Jesus, who do we choose - God, or things of this world?

> *Lord, when confronted with a choice, between a beaten God or a powerful king, let me choose you. A beaten God is more powerful than the greatest king in this world.*

JESUS IS LIFTED UP

Pilate then had Jesus crucified. Jesus took his cross and climbed the *"Place of a Skull"*. They crucified him with two others, one on each side. Pilate had a sign put on the cross *"JESUS OF NAZARETH, THE KING OF THE*

JEWS" in languages people in that land could understand. The leaders wanted that changed, but Pilate would not change it.

This proclamation was meant as a warning to those who wanted to incite rebellion. It was also meant to insult the Jews, to show the world how the Romans had again triumphed over their enemies.

Unknown to all of them, it also proclaimed the truth to the world - Jesus was (and still is) indeed, the King of the Jews. He was not a king of this world. He did not come to establish a kingdom on earth by political might. He came to establish a kingdom of heaven AND earth - by the power of God.

The soldiers divided his garment into four parts, but his coat, they cast lots for it. This was to fulfill scripture.

> *By your being lifted up Lord, you were proclaimed to the world as you really are, the true Savior! Come Lord, rule over my life.*

THE MOTHER OF JESUS

Jesus saw his mother and other women. He also saw his beloved disciple with them. Jesus gave the disciple first to his Mother, then he gave his Mother to the disciple. The disciple of Jesus was entrusted to the care of his Mother.

Mary is the Spouse of the Holy Spirit. Now that Jesus was dying, he will send the Holy Spirit. Mary will be the guide to her Son.

The disciple of Jesus obeys Jesus' Mother, trusts her and takes her home.

> *Mary, stay with me in my moments of despair. Mary, Mother of God, pray for me, a sinner. May I accept you as my Mother and take you to live with me.*

Catholics believe Mary remained a virgin throughout her life. This meant Jesus did not have any brothers born of Mary. This episode proves this. If Mary had children, those children would be responsible for taking care of their mother. However, Jesus gave Mary to the disciple to ensure she was cared for. John said, *"From that hour, the disciple took her to his own home."* This meant the disciple took care of Mary from that time.

THE SOURCE OF LIVING WATER THIRSTS

At the cross, Jesus said *"I thirst."* There was a vessel full of vinegar. They soaked a sponge and gave it to him. They gave him vinegar rather than water. The source of Living Water had emptied himself because he had poured himself out for the world. He gave up his spirit. Even here, Jesus was in control. He determined when he would die.

When Jesus died, the Law was powerless. The leaders did not want to break the Sabbath Law, so they asked the Romans to hasten the death of those crucified, by breaking their legs. When they came to Jesus, they saw he was dead so they did not break his bones. Instead, one of the soldiers made sure he was dead and pierced his side. Blood and water flowed out of this side. This proved Jesus was a human being, that he really died as a man.

> *Lord, by piercing your side, the soldier drained every last drop of blood from your body. You poured out your life for me. Thank you Jesus. I want to live for you Lord. I want to live in you. I want to live the life your Father has planned for me. Take me Jesus, make me yours for the glory of the Father.*

THE BURIAL OF JESUS

Joseph of Arimathaea came to Pilate and asked for the body of Jesus. He was a secret follower for fear of the

Jewish leaders. Pilate allowed him to take it. Nicodemus also came and brought expensive spices to anoint the body of Jesus. They bound the body. In the place where he was crucified was a garden with a tomb where no one had ever laid. They laid him there.

After the death at the skull, the body was laid in a garden. The seed was buried in a garden. The violence of death changed to the serenity of a garden. Adam lost his place in a garden and died. Jesus died to recover the garden. The seed must die and be buried so it may bear fruit. Jesus died and was buried so the Tree of Life may grow again.

> *Lord, restore to me the joy of your salvation. By your cross and resurrection, you have set me free, you are my Savior!*

Chapter 20

Joy after Sorrow

The chapter begins on the first day of the week, the first day of the new creation. Mary Magdalene went to the tomb and saw it empty. She ran back to tell Peter and the beloved disciple. They both ran to the tomb.

The beloved disciple outran Peter and arrived first. He bent down the tomb and looked inside. He saw the linen cloths but he stayed outside. Then Peter arrived and entered the tomb. He saw the linen cloth lying there and the cloth used to wrap Jesus' head was rolled up by itself. The disciple then entered. He saw and believed. They still did not know scripture and so did not know Jesus must rise from the dead.

The beloved disciple bent down and looked inside. He saw the cloths. Peter did not bend down but entered immediately and saw the linen cloths. The other disciple then went in and he saw and believed. There was no mention of Peter believing.

BELIEVING

The other disciple believed because he stooped down first before entering. Peter did not stoop down so he did not believe. To believe therefore, requires humility. One has to stoop down and experience the empty tomb.

Very often, I would not bend to the Lord's guiding hand. I would not want to go through difficulties. But when I do, I experience the empty tomb. I experience difficulties, to the point where God seems absent. Yet, it is through these difficult moments that faith is strengthened. When one experiences the empty tomb, the absence of God, then and only then will one believe in him.

> *Lord, teach me to humble myself. Teach me to believe in you even when things do not make sense. Jesus, teach me to remember your words.*

During these times, scripture would not matter. Nothing matters because nothing would make sense. The fact that Jesus is not where one expects him to be, is proof we are going towards a new life, a resurrected life.

After this, both men went back to their homes.

MARY SEES JESUS

Mary came back presumably with the two and stayed at the tomb, weeping. She stooped and looked inside and saw two angels inside the tomb. Mary stooped but stopped short of entering the tomb. They asked her why she was weeping. She thought someone had stolen Jesus' body. She did not wait for them to respond. She probably felt someone moving behind her. Jesus was standing there, but she did not recognize him.

He asked her, "*Woman, why are you weeping? Who are you looking for?*"

She thought he was the gardener and blamed him for stealing the body of Jesus. "*Sir, if you have carried him away, tell me where you have laid him, and I can take him away.*" Mary was before the risen Jesus, but she was still looking for the dead one. Worse, she even mistook the Risen One for a thief.

> *Lord, how often have I not trusted in you? Believing you will take away things I hold dear? Yet, in these times, you wanted to give me something more than what I had. You wanted to transform what I had. You wanted to perfect it. Teach me to trust in you.*

Jesus then spoke her name, *"Mary."* That was enough. She turned and she said, *"Teacher!"* Even if she did not recognize Jesus, she knew who the man was. She recognized him when he called her name.

"He calls his own sheep by name and he leads them out" (John 10:3). Mary was Jesus' sheep. She knew his voice. When Jesus called her name, he led her out of her grief.

First, she mistook Jesus as the gardener. In Genesis, man was created by God to take care of the garden. She mistook Jesus as still the fallen man. But he is risen and has now been glorified. He is the new Adam. He did not steal our inheritance, but he rose to give it back to us.

Do Not Hold Me

What is interesting is what Jesus said, *"Don't hold me, for I haven't yet ascended to my Father"*. When Mary recognized him, she immediately held him. Matthew's account said the women clasped his feet and worshiped him. The ascension of Jesus is the completion of his mission. He had to ascend to the Father so he could send the Holy Spirit.

Very often too, we continue to hold on to our image of the old Jesus. For one to grow and bear fruit, one must let go of what one thinks about him. Jesus is not the dead man. Jesus is the Risen One. He has risen and is victorious over death!

> *Lord, how many times have I tried to fit you into my image? How many times have I failed to accept you as you are? Come. Let me see you as you really are - the victorious God who rose from the dead! The God who loves me and saves me. The God who came to serve me and to die for me. The God who is victorious over all MY difficulties! Lord, come and lead me.*

Jesus continued, *"go to my brothers, and tell them, 'I am ascending to my Father and your Father, to my God and your God'."* With his resurrection, Jesus restored humanity to our original dignity. God became our Father. The fallen creation was redeemed.

Mary immediately ran off and told the disciples she had seen Jesus and all he told her.

This is what is required for those who have encountered the Risen Christ. One is called to go and tell others of the good news.

> *Lord, may I have the courage to go and tell others of this victorious news. Let me not keep this news to myself. Instead, help me to preach you, to speak of you to others. To speak of the wonderful things you have done for me.*

PEACE

The scene shifts to the evening. The disciples locked themselves in. They were still afraid of being arrested. Suddenly, Jesus appeared to them and stood among them and said, *"Peace be to you"*. This is a standard Jewish greeting.

He then showed them his hands and the pierced side. The disciples were glad when they saw Jesus. The Gospel of Luke said they could not believe because they were filled with joy and amazement.

Before they could say anything, Jesus again greeted them, *"Peace be to you."* He then commissioned them, *"As the Father has sent me, even so I send you. When he had said this, he breathed on them, and said to them, 'Receive the Holy Spirit! If you forgive anyone's sins, they have been forgiven them. If you retain anyone's sins, they have been retained'."*

In our grief and fear, we shut down. We raise our defenses. Yet, Jesus passes through all these. He stood before the Eleven (except Thomas) and he gave them his peace, twice!

When Jesus comes, he does not bring riches. He does not bring power. He brings his presence and peace. The presence of Jesus is enough because he is all that matters. Through our grief, through our miseries, through our sufferings, Jesus passes through them because he is greater than all these.

With Jesus, we have peace in the midst of all the troubles. Jesus said in John 14:27, *"Peace I leave with you. My peace I give to you; not as the world gives, give I to you. Don't let your heart be troubled, neither let it be fearful."*

This appearance of Jesus fulfills that promise. Troubles will come. Difficulties will come. We will have fears. But the important thing is Jesus is there. He will never leave us!

> *Lord, what a wondrous thought! The God of all creation cares for me. You have risen and instead of leaving us, you stayed and spoke to your people, giving them your peace. After giving us your life, you leave us your peace. Lord, what is there that you have not given us? Thank you Jesus.*

The Co-Mission

He then commissioned them as the Father had sent him. The Father sent his only begotten Son to die for the sin of the world - to conquer sin and redeem the world.

The same goes for us. We are sent to die to ourselves and to conquer sin. We are called to share in the threefold mission of Jesus: as a priest, as a king and as a prophet.

We are called to be priests - to pray for others and to offer ourselves as a living sacrifice, holy and pure, to heal and to give comfort. We are called to be kings to conquer sin within ourselves, to conquer evil within us and to show the world the power of God to change lives and uplift people from meaningless and defeated lives, to a life that is according to the will of God - victorious and glorious.

We are called to be prophets to preach the good news of the risen and victorious Jesus: that we have been restored our dignity as children of God.

> *Jesus, what have you done to me? I am sinful, yet, you have called me to share in your mission. You have restored to me my dignity as a child of God. Thank you Lord. Praise you Jesus for all the blessings you have given me. Thank you Lord for sharing your life. May I live my life according to your Father's will - to give him glory.*

Power Over Sin

To help the disciples to share in his mission, Jesus breathed on them. This breath is the Holy Spirit. He gives the Holy Spirit as a Counselor, a Defender and an Advocate. The Spirit of truth will guide us in all we do.

As he sent his disciples, the Holy Spirit was there to help them. The Holy Spirit gave them power to forgive sins. This meant the disciples of Jesus had authority over sin.

They had conquered sin, by the death of Jesus and they had power over it.

Very often, I hear people say Catholics have it easy. One can confess one's sins and the sins are forgiven. That is partly true. Yes, confession does wipe our sins away. But there is a condition to that. The person making the confession should have the desire to change.

If there is no desire to change, to repent, then there is no forgiveness of sin. The priest may say the words of absolution but the sins are not forgiven - because the person confessing has not accepted the forgiveness of Jesus.

Confession is a sacrament. It is our way of telling the Lord we want to have the victory he won for us. It is telling the Lord we want to live our lives as more than conquerors of sin. If one does not want to change, then where is the victory over sin? That person is still enslaved to sin. Therefore, the confession is not valid.

The desire to change is important. Due to human frailty, we will sin again. And that is what confession is all about. We want to change but we can't - not on our own. So we repeatedly come back to God for mercy and grace.

> *Lord Jesus, you have given me power over sin. Let me live my life in victory over sin. Let me live my life with the desire to conquer my sinfulness. Let me not take your death in vain. Change my heart O God.*

MY LORD AND MY GOD

The scene immediately switched to Thomas who was not there when Jesus first appeared. The disciples told him they had seen Jesus. But he would not believe until he saw the nail marks in Jesus' hands and put his hand in Jesus' side.

Eight days later, Jesus again appeared. This time Thomas was with them. Jesus specifically spoke to Thomas and told him to put his finger on his hands and put his hand into his side. Then Jesus told him, *"Don't be unbelieving, but believing."*

> *Lord, I want to believe. Help me in my unbelief.*

This second appearance was for the sake of Thomas. As one of the apostles, Thomas had to be convinced Jesus was alive. He was to be a witness of the resurrection.

Thomas did not even have to touch Jesus. He just said, *"My Lord and My God!"* He finally got it! He had seen Jesus, alive! He had experienced the Risen Jesus and that was enough for him.

There is this expression *"doubting Thomas"*, which I think is unfair to him. If one looks at it, all the apostles did not first believe until Jesus appeared to them. Thomas' fault was not that he did not believe. His fault was he was not there when Jesus first appeared!

THE RISEN JESUS

For one to fully know Jesus, one must experience the Risen Jesus. That is when one will realize he is truly divine. Until he saw the Risen Jesus, Thomas knew Jesus as a man. But when he saw the Risen Jesus, he called him God.

This is the first and only time, in this gospel, if not in the entire New Testament, when someone explicitly called Jesus as God. The closest they got was to call Jesus as the Son of God but none of them explicitly called him God. Thomas may have doubted, but he was the only one who expressed the truth clearly - Jesus is God.

> *Lord, how many times, I would not believe even when people tell me, or events would show me. Yet, in your mercy, you will do everything to convince me. Open my heart. Let me believe you have risen from the dead. I want to see you Lord. I want to see your glory. I want to experience the Risen Jesus so I can truly believe.*

The resurrection is the symbol of hope. It is our symbol of life. To believe in it leads to life.

BELIEVE WITHOUT SEEING

Jesus then told Thomas, *"Because you have seen me, you have believed. Blessed are those who have not seen, and have believed."*

For those who came after the first generation of disciples, we are blessed because we are able to believe even without seeing. This is not because we have more faith. It is because God has given us more grace to pierce through our stubborn hearts so we can believe.

The chapter ends by saying Jesus did many other things *"which are not written in this book"*. The things written in the book were included so those who read it may believe Jesus is the Son of God and in believing may have life in his name.

To have life, one must believe Jesus is the Son of God - he is fully human and fully divine. Everything depends on this belief.

> *Lord, you are the Son of God. May I respond to your grace as you reveal yourself to me. Break through my stubborn heart, O God. Guide me and lead me to you O Lord.*

Chapter 21

Follow Jesus

The chapter begins with an introduction saying Jesus revealed himself again by the sea of Tiberias. *"After these things, Jesus **revealed** himself again to the disciples at the sea of Tiberias. He **revealed** himself this way."*

The key word here is *reveal*. It is repeated twice. The one doing the revealing was Jesus.

Jesus is the only one who can reveal himself to us. By ourselves, we cannot know him.

The main point is Jesus wants to reveal himself to us. The question is: how do I respond to his revelation? Do I just brush him aside and go on doing my own thing? Or do I accept him at his word and seek him?

FRUITLESS WITHOUT JESUS

Seven disciples led by Peter were together. Peter said he was going fishing. The others joined him. John mentioned Peter on top of the list. This shows Peter in a leadership role in the community. They spent the whole night fishing and they caught nothing. Peter, an experienced fisherman, knew the best time to fish was in the evening, yet, he caught nothing.

In the morning, Jesus was on the beach but the disciples did not know it was him. Jesus asked them if they caught anything. He called them *"children"*. To Jesus, they were children in their new faith and they had to grow in their faith. They were also, children of God. As God, Jesus was claiming them as his own. They belonged to him.

> *Lord, many times, I have done things on my own. I have sought my own desires. In these, I have nothing to show. It is only in acknowledging you that I can truly bear fruit. Lord God, come to my life. Let me bear fruit for you - for the glory of the Father.*

ABUNDANCE!

Jesus told them to cast the net to the right side of the boat so they could catch fish. They obeyed, and now they caught a lot! They were not able to draw the catch in!

Several things need to be pointed out. Peter was a fisherman by trade, so were the two sons of Zebedee. They knew the best time to fish was in the evening. But despite their expertise, they could not catch anything. In the morning, when it was not the best time to fish, they just threw their nets carelessly at the word of Jesus, and they made a huge catch.

Two miracles happened here. The first was there was no fish in the evening when there should have been. The second was there was fish when there should not have been.

What does this mean?

God is full of surprises. It is a miracle even when we do not catch anything!

> *Lord, when I do not succeed despite my best efforts, let me know you are still there. Let me see your hand in my failures. Let me trust you through those failures. Let me allow you to lead me to deeper knowledge of you. This is all I need, this is all I want.*

In life, even if we are experts and skilled at something, we will not be fruitful without Jesus. John 15 says Jesus is the vine and we are the branches. If we do not remain in him, we will not bear fruit. To remain in Jesus is to obey, even if it does not make sense.

We should not trust in our own skills but instead, use our skills in union with God. The disciples had to use their skills with the net to still make the catch. The difference was in the evening, Jesus was not there.

SUPERABUNDANCE!

God gave us skills so we can use them for his glory. He tells us when AND where to use it.

In this case, he told the disciples to cast the net at the right side of the boat. We have to use our skills with Jesus; otherwise, we will not be able to fulfill what God had planned for us. We may succeed, but will always fall short of what God has planned for us.

Blessed Mother Teresa said *"I am not called to be successful. I am called to be faithful"*. We were not created to be successful. We were created to be glorious and great before God! This is achieved ONLY through faithfulness to God.

Of course God wants us to be successful! What parent would not want that for their children? But he wants more than that. He wants us to be great AND glorious, to enjoy the fullness of life!

This is why the catch was so much the disciples could not haul it in! God did not want them to catch a pittance. He wanted them to catch a lot - in superabundance!

God gives, and gives, and gives! He wants to give us a life that is full - and he still wants to fill it up to overflowing!

He is a superabundant God! His word ALWAYS brings superabundance!

How often Lord, have I gone my way, thinking it is what is best, without realizing you have planned the best for me. You want me to have a full and superabundant life! I want that life Lord! Let me use my skills and talents WITH you. Let me use these for your glory. Teach me to remain in you Lord Jesus so I may give glory to your Father.

GOING TO JESUS

When they had the catch, the beloved disciple knew it was Jesus and said that to Peter. When Peter was told it was Jesus, he wrapped his clothes and jumped into the water. I find this statement interesting. Why would someone put on his clothes to swim? Peter was naked, yet he put on his clothes so he could jump into the water.

This brings us back to the garden. The man and woman were naked and had to clothe themselves after they sinned. By doing so, Peter showed he was sinful. He had not heard Jesus' forgiveness yet.

Peter threw himself to the water as a sign of baptism. When he came up to the shore, you would expect him to be soaking wet. The author did not mention this. What he mentioned was when they came to the shore, they saw coal, bread and fish. The first thing Jesus told them was to bring some fish. Jesus had prepared some food. Yet, he asked them to bring some more fish.

God always has to prepare things for us so we can join him. Everything is God's initiative. But he wants us to be involved in his work.

Jesus could have prepared a meal for all of them, which he did, but he still asked them to bring what they caught.

> *Lord, in doing your work, let me wait for you to*
> *prepare things before I respond. Let me not go ahead*
> *of you. Let me follow you and wait for your leading.*
> *Lord, without you, I can do nothing.*

WORKING WITH GOD

Peter dragged the net and brought the catch to Jesus. Even though there were a lot of fish, the net was not torn.

God can work without us. He created the universe without us! But he wants us to participate in his saving work. We bring to him whatever he has made us catch. He prepares everything for us, but this does not mean there will be no difficulties. The disciples had to pull up the net from the water and drag it to the land. Peter had to drag the heavy net with fish so he could bring some to Jesus.

When Jesus told the disciples to bring some of the fish, John described what Peter did. He went up (presumably to the boat), drew the net to the land. Did he do this by himself with a net of more than one hundred fish? I don't think so. He needed the help of the disciples on the boat.

What does this mean? The command to bring some fish was to the disciples, but the focus was only on what Peter did. This shows Peter as the main character in this scene. Why not! He was the leader of the disciples. As such, he was the leader of the Church.

The net was heavy, yet it was not torn. The Church will have a lot of stress but it will never break. In Matthew's version of the gospel, Jesus said to Peter, "*I also tell you that you are Peter, and on this rock I will build my assembly, and the gates of Hades will not prevail against it.*" There will be problems from outside and inside the Church, but these will never prevail. It will never destroy the Church because Jesus said so.

> *Lord, you gave us your Church, with Peter as her head. Bless your Church. Bless our Pope so he may bring more people to know you. May he find courage and strength in you, for the glory of the Father. Bless our bishops and pastors. May they be truthful to your word. May they unite themselves to Peter on whom you built your Church.*

KNOWING JESUS

Throughout all their encounters with Jesus, the disciples did not recognize him, but they knew it was him.

This is an interesting fact recorded in all the versions of the gospel. It seems that after the resurrection, people did not recognize Jesus but still knew it was him.

In our life, we will know Jesus but will not be able to recognize him. We know he is working. We know he is moving. But we will still not recognize him - because it will be too marvelous for us to believe.

> *Lord, you did awesome things we did not expect. And you continue to do awesome things we will never expect!*

John says this was the third time Jesus was revealed. The word used again is *"revealed"*.

LOVING JESUS

After breakfast, Jesus asked Peter three questions; twice if he loved him unconditionally (the Greek word used comes from the word *agape*, meaning, to love unconditionally) and the last time if he had affection for him (the Greek word used comes from the word *phileo,* meaning, to love as a brother).

Agape is a love that is willed. It is an unconditional acceptance of a person. This is a decision. This is love for enemies.

Phileo is a narrower scope of love. It is more emotional. It is love for people who love us - like a love for brothers.

In those three times, Peter's response was he *phileo* Jesus - he loved Jesus as a brother. Peter could not admit he loved Jesus unconditionally. He knew he was weak and could fail just as he did before.

Three times Peter denied Jesus, three times Jesus allowed Peter to set things straight - and Peter did by admitting his weakness.

> *Lord, you are good. You accept me as I am. You love me for my weakness. Let me respond to you by acknowledging my weakness and return that love to you.*

Jesus did not hold that against Peter. He accepted Peter in his weakness. Every time Peter responded, Jesus entrusted the Church to him. Jesus does not demand that we become perfect immediately. He knows we are dust and he knows we will fail. But he accepts us where we are and from there, picks us up and leads us to perfection.

FOLLOW JESUS

After this, Jesus told Peter to follow him. We are all called to follow Jesus whatever our state is. This is difficult because we will be led to where we do not want to go.

This is part of being a disciple of Jesus. We will not be in control. Instead, we will be following where Jesus leads us. We will be followers rather than masters of our own destiny. Yet, by following Jesus, we reach the destiny he has planned for us - to be masters of all creation with him!

When Peter turned, he saw the Beloved Disciple following them. Peter asked Jesus about the disciple. Jesus told him quite bluntly, "*If I desire that he stay until I come, what is that to you? You follow me*." What Jesus does with the disciple was none of Peter's business. His business was to follow Jesus.

Our goal is to live a life with Jesus. How he deals with others is none of our business. For us, we follow Jesus the way he calls us.

Follow Jesus even if it does not make sense. Follow Jesus even if it is painful. Follow Jesus even if you are afraid. God is faithful. He will lead you through all difficulties. God is a God of victory. Be convinced of what Jesus said. Act on what he said and follow him. Believe to live!

This is the only way to victory. This is the only way to life!

Lord Jesus, you are the Son of the Living God. You have the words of eternal life, to whom should I go. I believe you are the Holy One of God. I surrender my life to you. Take, Lord. Receive. I give you permission to do with it as you wish. Transform it and may it be a sacrifice of praise, holy and pleasing to you.

Lead me to the life you have planned for me - to a life of victory; a life of glory with the Father. I want that life. Through difficulties and sufferings, I know you are with me - to lead me through. Be my strength and refuge O Lord.

Come Lord Jesus. Be the Lord of my life. I want to follow you. For me, it does not matter where I go as long as I know I am following you. This is enough for me Lord.

Holy Spirit, come. Breathe in me and unleash your power in my life. I want to live for Jesus, for the glory of the Father.

Mary, my Mother, pray for me. Lead me to your Son, Jesus Christ my Lord!

Glory to the Father, and to the Son and to the Holy Spirit. As it was in the beginning, is now and ever shall be world without end.

Amen!

Epilogue

My reflections end here. The important thing about scripture is not in understanding it. It is in believing and living it.

The gospel writer said the purpose for writing the gospel was *"that you may believe that Jesus is the Christ, the Son of God, and that believing you may have life in his name."*

I pray this book was able to help instill that desire in you to learn more about the life God has planned for you. The only way to know this life is through Jesus. I pray in the coming days, you will be able to learn about him and learn from him.

God is good! He has given us everything we need! St. Paul said in Ephesians 1:3 *"Blessed be the God and Father of our Lord Jesus Christ, who has blessed us with every spiritual blessing in the heavenly places in Christ ."* God gave us all we need. Every spiritual blessing we need has been given to us even before anything was created! Now THAT is something to think about!

This is our God! Such is his love!

All we need to do is to take these blessings and graces to know Jesus. We do not ask for the grace to know Jesus since God has already given that to us. We need to respond to his invitation, to have the courage to respond to him in love.

God is a personal God. He reveals himself to us based on our needs because everyone is unique. May the Lord bless us all and may we all strive to live our lives according to his will.

May we all respond to his invitation to a full life - a life with him and may we all see each other in our life with him for all eternity.

May God be glorified in all we do - through Jesus Christ our Lord!

Manufactured by Amazon.ca
Bolton, ON

33281257R00077